뉴 통번역연습

한울출판사

머리말
PREFACE

외국어를 공부하는 데 있어 듣기(Listening)만 따로 떼어내서 공부할 수 없는 것은 그것이 읽기(Reading), 말하기(Speaking), 쓰기(Writing)와 서로 연결되어 있기 때문이다. 독해에 능숙한 사람이 듣기도 잘하고, Listening에 능숙한 사람이 Speaking도 잘하고 아울러 통역도 정확히 잘 할 수 있다. Listening이 안 되는 사람은 Speaking도 잘 할 수 없고 또한 통역도 잘 할 수 없다. 따라서 영어를 공부할 때 듣기 따로 읽기 따로 말하기 따로 하는 공부는 별 의미가 없다. 리스닝 학습을 할 때는 읽기, 말하기, 쓰기가 병행되어야 한다.

영어 리스닝에서의 최대 난점은 쉬운 영어라도 원어민의 속도를 따라가는 것이 힘들다는 점이다. 또한 알아들은 영어라도 그 어순을 우리말식으로 바꿔놓고 해석할 수 있는 시간적 여유가 없다는 것이다. 그래서 도입된 훈련법이 바로 동시 통역사들이 훈련하는 직청직해 훈련법이다. 영어의 어순은 누가, 무엇을 했다는 말이 먼저 나오고, 그 다음 '무엇을'에 해당하는 정보가 나오는데, 이렇게 영어가 들리는 대로 의미 단위 또는 사고 단위마다 끊어서 번역해 가는 것이 직청직해이다. 이런 번역을 동시 통역사들은 '순차번역'이라고도 한다. 이렇게 영어가 들리는 대로, 즉 영어의 어순대로 의미 단위로 이해하는 직청직해식(Chunk and Chew)훈련을 쌓게 되면 영어식 어순 감각을 익히게 되어, 영어식으로 사고하고 말하고 쓰는데 아주 큰 도움이 된다.

미국의 여러 방송국 간판 앵커들의 정확한 발음과 표준 억양을 접하기는 그리 쉬운 일은 아니다. 그래서 이러한 뉴스를 집중적으로 청취하면 영어실력이 대단히 향상된다고 확신한다. CD를 통해 가능한 한 많이 들어서 원어민의 속도대로 이해하면 직청직해에 능숙해지고, 또한 많이 따라 하다보면 영어의 리듬을 익힐 수 있다. 바로 이 책은 그 영어의 리듬을 익히도록 구성했다. Dictation 부분을 인쇄하여 빈칸 채워 넣는 연습을 할 수 있도록 만들었다. 정확한 리스닝을 위해서는 받아쓰기를 해야 한다. 끝으로 이 책을 통하여 영어통역연습을 많이 할 수 있기를 바라는 마음 간절하다.

2010년 12월

박 노철

C·O·N·T·E·N·T·S

01

Dangerous Collision airplanes and geese

Flight risk. A close call for a jumbo jet proves again airplanes and geese in the same airspace are a bad mix. But what to do about it?

There has been another close call involving a commercial airliner, a jumbo jet, this time and a flock of geese. This one happened in the skies over New Jersey . Witnesses describe the collision as loud and terrifying.

A reminder of the danger of birds and plane sharing the same airspace.

The story tonight from NBC's Tom Costello.

It was a harrowing 90 minutes Wednesday for the 301 people on board a fully loaded jumbo jet.

Continental flight 99 from Newark to Hong Kong left at 6:31 and was only 300 feet in the air when it ran into a flock of Canada geese immediately raising concern that the plane's engines might not make it the 16 hours to Asia.
The radar track shows the Boeing 777 circling over New Jersey for nearly 90 minutes while it dumped jet fuel before landing safely back at Newark.
The fuel mist evaporating in the sky.

Retired 777 captain Tom Casing knows about dumping 137,000 pounds of fuel.
He once, had to aboard a New York to Tokyo flight.
“If you have to come back, you have to land light because the plane can't take a landing at those heavy weights. 100⋯...200,000 pounds of fuel.”
Last year's miracle on the Hudson flight drove home to bird risk after geese took out both engines.
In the first nine months of 2009, reports of bird strikes were up 24% to just over 7,200.
But that sudden jump is largely because of better reporting.

While the geese population is exploding, wild life experts insist loud cannons, bird trapping egg and nest removals have already make airports much safer.
“But I think the threat is growing outside of the airport environment.”
That's what happened in November as Frontier Flight 820 departed Kansas City for Denver.
“Mayday, Mayday, Frontier 820, multiple bird strikes.”
Frontier 820 landed safely on one engine.

To deal with the out of airport threat, airports are now experimenting with bird radar to guide planes around large flocks and also putting strobe lights on planes to scare birds away, all in an effort to reduce costly and potentially deadly encounters in the skies.

Tom Costello, NBC News, Washington.

Words and Idioms

- close call 위기일발
  - The speeding taxi nearly hit him; that was a **close call**.
  - The women are talking about a **close call**.
- harrowing 괴로운, 끔찍한, 참혹한
  - The sight was too **harrowing** to look at.
    그 광경은 차마 볼 수 없을 만큼 애처로운 것이었다.
- mist 안개, 이슬 눈물이 맺히다.
  - The origins of the story are lost in the **mists** of time.
    그 이야기의 기원은 시간의 안개 속에 사라져 버렸다.
  - Her eyes **misted over** as she listened to the speech.
    그녀는 그 연설을 들으면서 눈에 이슬이 맺혔다.
- evaporate 증발하다[시키다]/ 차츰 사라지다
  - Heat until all the water has **evaporated**.
    수분이 모두 증발할 때까지 열을 가하라.
  - Her confidence had now completely **evaporated**.
    그녀는 이제 자신감이 완전히 사라져 버린 상태였다.

- Last year's miracle on the Hudson flight **drove home** to bird risk after geese took out both engines.
  - drive home은 '납득 / 인식시키다, (일) 핵심을 찌르다'를 의미하고, take out은 '(물고기, 새) 걸리다, 잡히다 등'을 나타낸다.

- All in an effort to reduce costly and potentially deadly encounters in the skies.
  - reduce(줄이다)는 앞에 위치한 명사 effort을 수식하는 to 부정사의 형용사적 용법으로 쓰였다.

번역 기러기, 여객기와 충돌 위험

비행 위험에 관한 소식입니다. 점보제트기의 위기일발 순간은 다시한번 동일한 항공영역에서 비행기와 기러기가 좋지 못한 궁합을 이룬다는 사실을 증명합니다. 이에 관해 무엇을 해야 할까요?
이번에는 상업용 여객기 즉, 점보제트기와 기러기 떼를 포함한 위기일발의 순간이 있었습니다. 이번 사건은 뉴저지주 상공에서 발생했습니다.
목격자에 따르면 해당 충돌 사건이 큰 굉음을 냈고 무서웠다고 합니다.
동일한 항공영역을 공유하는 새들과 비행기의 위험성을 일깨워줍니다.
오늘 저녁, NBC 뉴스의 톰 코스텔로 기자가 보도합니다.

수요일 승객을 가득 실은 점보제트기에 탑승한 301 명에게는 괴로웠던 90분이었습니다.
뉴어크 - 홍콩 행 콘티넨탈 항공 99는 6시 31분에 이륙한 뒤 겨우 300 피트 상공에 떠 있었습니다. 이때 비행기는 캐나다 기러기 떼와 부딪히자 이내 비행기 엔진이 아시아까지 16시간 동안 무사히 비행하지 못할지도 모른다는 염려가 생겼습니다.
레이더 추적은 보잉 777이 뉴어크에 무사히 다시 착륙하기 이전, 비행기가 제트기 연료를 쏟아내는 동안 약 90분가량 뉴저지 상공에서 원을 그리는 모습을 보여줍니다.
연료(안개)는 하늘에서 증발했습니다.

은퇴한 보잉 777기장인 톰 케이싱씨는 137,000파운드의 연료를 쏟아 붓는 것이 어떤 것인지 잘 알고 있습니다.
그는 뉴욕 - 도쿄 행 비행기를 운항해야 했습니다.
"다시 되돌아가야 할 경우에는 비행기를 가볍게 착륙시켜야 합니다. 비행기는 그렇게 무거운 무게로 착륙할 수 없기 때문입니다. 10만 …20만 파운드가량의 연료가 해당됩니다."
작년 '허드슨강의 기적(a miracle on the Hudson)'의 비행기는 거위가 두 엔진에 걸려든 일이 있은 뒤 조류 위험성을 이해시켰습니다.
2009년 첫 9개월간 조류 충돌에 관한보고는 24% 상승했고 7,200건이 넘었습니다.
한편, 갑작스럽게 수치가 뛴 것은 대부분 보고를 더 잘했기 때문입니다.

기러기 개체수가 폭발적으로 증가하는 한편 기러기 야생동물 전문가들은 소리가 큰 대포, 조류용 덫, 알과 둥지 제거가 이미 공항을 훨씬 더 안전하게 했다고 주장합니다.
"이 같은 위협이 공항환경 외부에서 증가하고 있다고 봅니다."
바로 11월 덴버 행 프론티어 항공 820이 켄사스시를 출발할 때 일어난 발생했던 사건입니다.
"구조요청, 구조요청(주 _Mayday는 항공기의 구조요청 신호임), 프론티어 820기가 여러 번 조류와 충돌했다."
한편, 프론티어 820은 엔진 하나로 안전하게 착륙했습니다.
공항 외부에서 일어나는 위협을 다루기 위해 공항 측은 대규모 조류 떼 주변 비행기를 안내하기 위해 현재 조류레이더로 실험 중이며, 또한 조류를

겁주어 쫓아내기 위해 비행기에 플래시 라이트를 설치했습니다.
상공에서 희생이 크고 잠재적으로 일어날 수 있는 치명적인 충돌을 줄이기 위한 노력입니다.
워싱턴에서 NBC 뉴스 톰 코스텔로 기자였습니다.

Dictation

- Flight risk. ____ close call ______ ____ jumbo jet proves ________
- airplanes ______ geese ____ ______ same airspace ______ ____ bad mix. ______ ________ ____ do ________ ____?
- __________ ______ ________ ________ close call involving ____ commercial airliner, ____ jumbo jet, ________ ______
- ______ ____ flock ____ geese. ________ one happened ____ ______ skies over New Jersey.
- Witnesses describe ______ collision ____ loud ______ terrifying.
- ____ reminder ____ ______ danger ____ birds ______ plane sharing ______ same airspace.
- ______ story tonight ________ NBC's Tom Costello.
- ____ ______ ____ harrowing 90 minutes Wednesday ______ ______ 301 people ____ board ____ fully loaded jumbo jet.

- Continental flight 99 _______ Newark ___ Hong Kong left ___ 6:31 _____ _____ only 300 feet ___ _____ air
- _____ ___ ran _____ ___ flock ___ Canada geese
- immediately raising concern _______ _____ plane's engines might not make ___ _____ 16 hours ___ Asia.
- _____ radar track shows _____ Boeing 777
- circling over New Jersey _____ nearly 90 minutes _______ ___ dumped jet fuel
- _______ landing safely _______ ___ Newark.
- _____ fuel mist evaporating ___ _____ sky.
- Retired 777 captain Tom Casing knows _______ dumping 137,000 pounds ___ fuel.
- _______ once, _____ ___ aboard ___ New York ___ Tokyo flight.
- “If _____ _________ ___ come _______, _____ _________ ___ land light because _____ plane _____'t _________ ___ landing ___ _________ heavy weights.
- 00⋯...200,000 pounds ___ fuel.”
- _______ _______’s miracle ___ _____ Hudson flight drove home ___ bird risk after geese took _____ both engines.
- ___ _____ _______ nine _________ ___ 2009, reports ___ bird strikes were ___ 24% ___ _____ over 7,200.

- _____ _______ sudden jump ___ largely because ___ better reporting.
- _______ _____ geese population ___ exploding, wild life experts insist
- loud cannons, bird trapping egg _____ nest removals _________ already make airports much safer.
- "_____ ___ _______ _____ threat ___ growing outside ___ _____ airport environment."
- _____________ _______ happened ___ November ___ Frontier Flight 820 departed Kansas City _____ Denver.
- "Mayday, Mayday, Frontier 820, multiple bird strikes." Frontier 820 landed safely ___ one engine.
- ___ deal _______ _____ _____ ___ airport threat, airports _____ now experimenting _______ bird radar ___ guide planes around large flocks
- _____ also putting strobe lights ___ planes ___ scare birds away,
- _____ ___ ___ effort ___ reduce costly _____ potentially deadly encounters ___ _____ skies.
- Tom Costello, NBC News, Washington.

02

Mexicans fled to the US due to gangsters

The drug war south of the border.

It's driving Mexicans north from one of the most dangerous cities on earth to one of the safest.

While President Obama was signing the healthcare law today, several top administration officials flew to Mexico City for a drug summit, led by Secretary of State Hilary Clinton and Defense Secretary Robert Gates.

And the US team promised Mexico long term support for its war on the drug cartels. One of the front lines is the border city of Juarez.

And Bill Wittker tells us, thousands are leaving there heading north to escape the violence.

Luis Aril Anzures is 29 and a successful restaurateur in El Paso, Texas.

But 11 months ago, he lived across the border in Juarez, Mexico, one of the most dangerous cities on earth.

One day driving home, three cars surrounded him.
"People came out of the cars with AK 47s told me to get out of the car, made me kneel down on the street . I thought I was going to die."
That moment soldiers drove up and saved him.
That night, Luis and his family fled to El Paso, one of the safest cities in the US just 13 murders last year.

They now have a thriving new restaurant and a safe new life. "We love it here."
He's part of a growing number of people fleeing north to safety across the Rio Grande.
This is one of the busiest ports along the border, 23 million people cross back and forth each year.
But in the past two years, as many as 80,000 people have crossed from Juarez to El Paso and not gone back.
Now one of every 15 El Paso residents is believed to be a recent transplant from Juarez, the upper middle class with visas, green cards or dual citizenships.

And this is what they're fleeing.
Americans Leslie Enriquez and Arthur Redelfs killed in a Juarez drive - by shooting 11 days ago, are two of 600 drug gang killings so far this year, almost 2,600 last year.

Gangsters are killing to control this lucrative drug smuggling route to the US.
University of Texas, El Paso professor Tony Payan is writing a book on Juarez. "The young people, the talented people, the engineers, the nurses, the doctors are simply leaving the city."
Bringing an economic boost to El Paso.
The last time so many affluent Mexicans fled their country was during the Mexican revolution 100 years ago. Harry?
Bill Wittker in El paso tonight. Thanks.

Words and Idioms

- thriving 번성[번영]하는, 번화한; 성대한/〈동식물이〉잘 자라는, 무성한
  - In schools across the U.S. young boys are falling behind, while young girls are **thriving.**
    미국 전역의 학교들에서 여자 아이들이 월등한 성적을 나타내는 반면 남자 아이들은 뒤처지고 있습니다.
- flee 달아나다, 도망하다
  - She burst into tears and **fled.**
    그녀는 울음을 터뜨리며 달아났다.
- lucrative 수익성이 좋은
  - This is a very **lucrative** business.
- affluent 부유한
  - He lives in an **affluent** suburb with large houses.
    그는 큰 집들이 있는 부유한 교외에 산다.

- It's driving Mexicans north **from one of the most dangerous cities on earth to one of the safest.**
  - from A to B 는 'A에서 B 까지'이고, **on earth**는 지상에서라는 의미로 최상급을 강조할 때 쓰인다.
- He's part of **a growing number of people** fleeing north to safety across the Rio Grande.
  - [a number of + 복수명사]는 '다수의 (many)'를 나타내며 여기에서 전치사 of 는 '~중의, ~의 일부'를 표현한다.

번역 멕시코인 미국으로 이주, 갱단피해서

국경 남쪽의 마약 전쟁입니다.
이 사건은 멕시코 인들을 지구상에서 가장 위험한 도시 중 하나인 북부 지역에서 가장 안전한 지역 중 한 곳으로 이동시키고 있습니다.
오늘 오바마 대통령이 건강보험 법안에 서명하는 한편, 고위급 행정 관료들 일부가 마약 회담을 위해 멕시코시티로 갔습니다. 이 회담은 힐러리 국무장관과 로버트 게이츠 국방장관 주도로 이루어졌습니다.
또한, 미국 대표들은 멕시코에 마약 카르텔에 맞선 장기적 지원을 약속했습니다.
최전선 중 한 곳은 국경도시 후아레스입니다.
수천 명이 폭력 사태를 피하기 위해 북으로 향해 떠나고 있는 사실에 대해 빌 위트커 기자가 보도합니다.

루이스 아릴 안주어스씨는 29세로 텍사스주 엘파소의 성공적인 레스토랑 운영자입니다.

하지만 11개월 전 그는 지구상에서 가장 위험한 도시 중 한 곳인 멕시코 후아레스의 국경 너머에 살았습니다.
어느 날 운전하며 집으로 가던 중, 자동차 3 대가 그를 둘러쌌습니다.
"사람들이 AK 47 소총을 들고 자동차 밖으로 나와 저보고 차 밖으로 나가라고 했습니다. 그리고 길거리에서 무릎을 꿇게 했습니다. 전 이제 죽겠구나 싶었죠."
그 순간 군인들이 차를 몰고 와 그를 구해줬습니다.
그날 저녁, 루이스와 가족들은 엘파소로 도망갔습니다. 작년 한해 살인사건이 겨우 13건만 일어난 가장 안전한 도시 중 하나였습니다.

그들은 지금 장사가 잘되는 새로운 레스토랑이 있고 안전한 삶을 살고 있습니다. "우리는 이곳이 마음에 듭니다."
그는 리오그란데를 넘어 안전을 위해 북쪽으로 이주하는 수많은 사람들 중 일부입니다.
이곳은 국경을 따라 위치하나 가장 분주한 항구 중 하나입니다. 매년 2,300명가량이 여기저기 넘나듭니다.
그러나 지난 2년간 약 8만 명이 후아레스에서 엘파소로 넘어왔고 되돌아가지 않았습니다.
현재 엘파소 거주자 15명 중 1명꼴로 비자, 그린카드 또는 이중국적을 가진 중산층으로 후아레스에서 최근 이주한 것으로 여겨집니다.

이것이 그들이 이주하는 이유입니다.
11일전 지나치던 차량에 총격을 당해 사망한 미국인 레슬리 엔리케즈와 아더 렌델크는 올해 지금까지 마약 갱단에 의해 죽은 600명 중 두 명이며, 작년에는 약 2,600명이 사망했습니다.
갱단은 돈벌이가 되는 미국의 마약 밀매 루트를 통제하기 위해 사살하고 있습니다.

엘파소주 텍사스 대학의 토니 파이안 교수는 후아레스에 관한 글을 집필하고 있습니다.
"젊은이들, 인재들, 엔지니어, 간호사 및 의사들이 그 도시를 떠나고 있습니다."
엘파소에 경기부양을 가져오고 있습니다.
상당히 많은 부유한 멕시코 인들이 자국을 떠난 가장 최근 시기는 100년 전 멕시코 혁명기 동안이었습니다. 해리?
오늘 저녁, 엘파소에서 빌 위트커 기자가 보도했습니다. 고맙습니다.

Dictation

- _____ drug war south ___ _____ ________.
- _____ driving Mexicans north _______ one ___ _____ _______ dangerous cities ___ _______ ___ one ___ _____ safest.
- _______ President Obama _____ signing _____ healthcare law today,
- several top administration officials flew ___ Mexico City _____ ___ drug summit,
- _______ ___ Secretary ___ State Hilary Clinton _____ Defense Secretary Robert Gates.
- _____ _____ US _______ promised Mexico long _______ support _____ _________ war ___ _____ drug cartels.
- One ___ _____ front lines ___ _____ ________ city ___ Juarez.

- ______ Bill Wittker ________ us, thousands ______ leaving __________ heading north ____ escape ______ violence.
- Luis Aril Anzures ____ 29 ______ ____ successful restaurateur ____ El Paso, Texas.
- ______ 11 __________ ago, ________ lived ________ ______ _________ ____ Juarez, Mexico, one ____ ______ ________ dangerous cities ____ ________.
- One day driving home, _________ ________ surrounded ________.
- People came ______ ____ ______ ________ ________ AK 47s told me ____ ______ ______ ____ ______ car,
- ________ me kneel down ____ ______ ________ . ____ thought ____ ______ __________ ____ die."
- ________ moment soldiers drove ____ ______ ________ ________.
- ________ night, Luis ______ ________ ________ ________ ____ El Paso, one ____ ______ safest cities ____ ______ US ______ 13 murders ________ ________.
- __________ now __________ ____ thriving new restaurant ______ ____ safe new life. "We love ____ ________ . "
- ________'s part ____ ____ growing number ____ people fleeing north ____ safety ________ ______ Rio Grande.
- ________ ____ one ____ ______ busiest ports ________ ______ _________, 23 __________ people cross ________ ______ forth each _______.

- _____ ___ _____ past two years, ___ _______ ___ 80,000 people ________ crossed _______ Juarez ___ El Paso _____ not gone _______.
- Now one ___ every 15 El Paso residents ___ believed ___ _______ ___ recent transplant _______ Juarez ,
- _____ upper middle class _______ _______, green cards ___ dual citizenships.
- _____ _______ ___ _______ _____________ fleeing .
- Americans Leslie Enriquez _____ Arthur Redelfs killed ___ ___ Juarez drive - ___ shooting 11 days ago,
- _____ two ___ 600 drug gang killings ___ ________ _______ _______, almost 2,600 _______ _______.
- Gangsters _____ killing ___ control _______ lucrative drug smuggling route ___ _____ US.
- University ___ Texas, El Paso professor Tony Payan ___ writing ___ book ___ Juarez.
- "_____ young people, _____ talented people, _____ engineers, _____ nurses, _____ doctors _____ simply leaving _____ city."
- Bringing ___ economic boost ___ El Paso.
- _____ _______ _____ ___ _______ affluent Mexicans _______ _______ country _____ during _____ Mexican revolution 100 years ago. Harry?
- Bill Wittker ___ El paso tonight. Thanks.

03

Poland's highest leaders were killed in a fiery presidential plane

The president of Poland, the first lady, the country's chief of staff and some of Poland's highest ranking military and civilian leaders, all killed in a fiery plane crash in Russia.
New details tonight on this developing story, I am Harris Volker in for Julie Vanderas.
This is Fox report.

We're told the plane burst into flames just moments after trying to land in what's described as dense fog, leaving no survivors.

And now we're learning air traffic controllers reportedly told the pilot to land somewhere else.

But those warnings were apparently ignored.

Tonight, a nation in mourning as investigators search for answers.

Good morning, breaking news, air disaster!

A jetliner carrying 96 people crashes while trying to land in thick fog, killing everyone on board including the president of Poland.

Adoption nightmare!

Why would an adopted parent here in America sent little boy back to his home country, half way around the world all by himself?

And wedding bells. Is Elizabeth Tayor planning another trip down the aisle?

Reports of what could lucky number 9.

Today Saturday April 10th, 2010. From NBC News, this is TODAY with Lestor Holt and Amy Robach, live from studio 1A in Rockefeller Plaza.

Good morning, everyone welcome to Today on this Saturday morning, I'm Lester Holt and I'm Amy Rock and it's nice to have you back Lester.

Well another breaking new story we've been following this morning.

The president of Poland is among those who died today when a Polish jetliner crashed on landing in Russia!

All 96 people on board were killed.

NBC's TOM ASPELL joins us now from LONDON with the latest. Tom, good morning!

Good morning, Amy, The TUPLOP 154 airplane crashed in thick fog in Russia killing all 96 people on board including Polish President LECH KASINSKI and his wife MARIA.

Local official said the airplane caught fire after it hit the ground.

Rescue teams attempted to pull passengers out of the wreckage, but there were no survivors.

Words and Idioms

- civilian 민간인
  - The military government was refusing to transfer power to the **civilian** government.
    군사 정부는 민간 정부에 권력을 넘기려고 하지 않았다
  - A **civilian** with no experience cracked a murder case in an unfamiliar city.
    경험도 없는 한 민간인이 낯선 도시에서 발생한 살인사건을 해결했다.
- burst into (갑자기) ~을 터뜨리다[내뿜다]
  - She **burst into** tears when she heard her old friend's death.
    그녀는 오랜 친구의 죽음을 전해 듣고 울음을 터뜨렸다.
  - Mr. Farland was so impressed by the ruling that he **burst into** tears in the courtroom.
    파랜드씨는 판결에 감동해 법정에서 눈물을 터뜨렸습니다.
- mourn (사람의 죽음을) 애도하다; 애석해 하다
  - He was still **mourning** his brother's death.
    그는 아직도 형[남동생]의 죽음을 슬퍼하고 있었다.

- They **mourn** the passing of a simpler way of life.
  그들은 더 소박한 삶의 방식이 사라지는 것을 애석해 한다.

• wreckage (사고 자동차, 비행기 등의) 잔해

- A few survivors were pulled from the **wreckage**.
  사고 잔해 속에서 몇 명의 생존자들이 끌려나왔다.
- Pieces of **wreckage** were found ten miles away from the scene of the explosion.
  폭발 현장으로부터 10마일 떨어진 곳에서 잔해 조각들이 발견되었다.

• And wedding bells. Is Elizabeth Tayor planning another trip down the aisle?

: walk down the aisle은 신랑, 신부가 결혼식이 끝난 후 통로로 나오는 모습을 나타낸다. 여기에서는 동사를 trip(경쾌한 걸음걸이로 걷다)이라는 단어로 표현했다.

• Rescue teams attempted to pull passengers out of the wreckage, but there were no survivors.

: attempt(=try) 는 to 부정사를 사용하여 '시도하다, 애를 쓰다'는 의미를 갖는다. 같은 표현으로 make an attempt가 있다. pull something out of 는 '~을 끄집어내다, 끌어내다'는 뜻이다.

번역 폴란드 대통령 전용기 추락, 전원 사망

러시아에서 비행기 충돌 사고로 폴란드 대통령, 영부인, 고위급 공무원, 참모총장 및 민간 지도자 전원이 사망했습니다.
오늘 저녁, 진행 중인 사건 소식에 관해 자세한 내용을 전해드리겠습니다.
저는 줄리 반데라스 앵커 대신 진행을 맡은 해리 볼커입니다.

폭스 리포트입니다.

당시 안개가 짙게 낀 상태에서 착륙을 시도한 직후 비행기가 화염에 휩싸였고, 생존자가 한 사람도 없었다는 사실을 들었습니다.
항공교통 관제사들의 보도에 따르면 담당 조종사에게 다른 지역에 착륙하라는 지시를 내렸다고 합니다. 그러나 이 같은 경고는 명백하게 무시됐습니다.
오늘 저녁, 조사관들이 해답을 얻기 위해 조사를 착수하자 한 국가가 비탄에 빠졌습니다.

안녕하십니까, 속보입니다. 비행기 참사 소식입니다.
승객 96 명을 태운 제트여객기가 짙은 안개 속에서 착륙을 시도하다가 충돌하여 폴란드 대통령 등 탑승객 전원이 사망했습니다.
입양 악몽 소식입니다!
왜 이곳 미국의 입양 부모가 아이 혼자서 지구 반바퀴를 돌아가야 하는 아이의 본국으로 돌려보냈을까요?
웨딩 벨이 울릴까요? 엘리자베스 테일러가 또 다른 결혼식을 계획하고 있는 것일까요?
아홉 번째 행운의 주인공이 누가 될지 보도합니다.
오늘은 2010년 4월 10일 토요일입니다. NBC 뉴스에서 레스터 홀트와 에이미 로박 앵커가 진행하는 〈TODAY〉입니다. 록펠러 플라자의 1A 스튜디오에서 생방송으로 보내드립니다.

안녕하십니까? 이번 주 토요일 아침 〈TODAY〉에 오신 것을 환영합니다. 저는 레스터 홀트입니다.
그리고 저는 에이미 로박입니다. 그리고 다시 레스터 앵커를 모시게 돼 기쁩니다.
오늘 아침 계속 이어지는 또 다른 새로운 속보입니다.

오늘 러시아에서 폴란드 제트 여객기가 착륙 도중 추락했을 당시 사망자 가운데 폴란드 대통령이 있었습니다.
탑승객 96명 전원이 사망했습니다.
최신 뉴스를 가지고 NBC 의 톰 애스펠 기자가 함께 해 주시겠습니다. 톰 기자, 안녕하십니까?

에이미 앵커, 안녕하세요? 러시아의 짙은 안개 속에서 투폴레프 (TU)-154 비행기가 추락하여, 레흐 카친스키 폴란드 대통령과 마리아 카친스키 영부인을 포함한 탑승객 96명 전원이 사망했습니다.
현지 공무원에 따르면 비행기가 땅에 부딪힌 뒤 불이 붙었다고 합니다.
구조대원들이 비행기 잔해에서 승객들을 끌어내려고 시도했지만 생존자는 한 명도 없었습니다.

Dictation

- The president's Poland , the first lady, the country's ________ ________ staff and some ________ Poland 's highest ranking military
- and civilian leaders, all killed ______ a fiery plane ________ ______ Russia.
- New details tonight ________ this ___________ story, I am Harris Volker ______ ________ Julie Vanderas.
- This ________ Fox report.
- We're told the plane ________ ________ ___________.
- just moments after trying _______ land ______ what's described ________

__________ __________, leaving no survivors.

- And now we're learning air traffic controllers reportedly told the __________ ______ land somewhere else.
- But __________ warnings __________ ___________ ___________.
- Tonight, a nation _____ __________ _______ ___________ search _______ answers.
- Good morning, __________ news, air __________!
- A jetliner carrying 96 people ___________ while trying ______ land _____ __________ __________,
- killing everyone _______ ___________ __________ the president _______ Poland .
- Adoption nightmare! Why _________ an adopted parent here _____ America ______ little boy ______ ______ his home country,
- __________ way __________ the world all _______ __________?
- And wedding bells. _______ Elizabeth Tayor planning another __________ __________ the __________?
- Reports _______ what __________ lucky number 9.
- Today Saturday April 10 th , 2010. From NBC News, this _______ TODAY with Lestor Holt and Amy Robach, live from studio 1A _____ Rockefeller Plaza.
- Good morning, everyone welcome ______ Today _______ this Saturday

morning, I'm Lester Holt

- and I'm Amy Rock and it's nice ______ have you ______ Lester.
- Well another _________ new story _________ _________ _________ this morning.
- The president _______ Poland _______ _________ _________ _________ died today when a Polish jetliner _________ _______ landing _____ Russia!
- All 96 people _______ __________ _________ killed.
- NBC's TOM ASPELL joins us now from LONDON with the latest. Tom, good morning!
- Good morning, Amy, The TUPLOP 154 airplane _________ _____ _________ _________ _____ Russia killing all 96 people _______ _________
- _________ Polish President LECH KASINSKI and his wife MARIA.
- _________ _________ said the airplane _________ _________ after it hit the ground.
- Rescue teams attempted ______ _________ passengers _________ _______ the _________, but there _________ no survivors.

04

The worst mining disaster in West Virginia

On our broadcast here tonight, desperate hours at that mine disaster in West Virginia and amid the staggering death toll, new questions now about the mining company's safety record. Nightly News begins now. From NBC News world headquarters in New York, this is NBC Nightly News with Brian Williams.

Good evening. it was a catastrophic explosion deep underground and the loss of life is staggering, even for the coal mining industry in West Virginia that has seen so much tragedy over the years. Tonight, 25 miners are dead. Another 4 are still missing. There's a herculean and urgent effort under way by rescuers to drill several holes as deep as 1,200 feet down to release trapped gas inside the mine.

I'm Harry Smith in Montcoal, West Virginia, home to the Big Branch Mine where yesterday a devastating explosion took the lives of 25 men. 18 bodies are still trapped inside and 4 miners are still unaccounted for. But the air inside the mineshaft is so poisonous. Rescue work is impossible. So family and friends are trapped, too, between hope and despair. This is the CBS Evening News with Katie Couric, tonight Harry Smith reporting tonight from the site of the mine disaster in West Virginia.

Good evening. Katie is on assignment. Well, it has been more than 24 hours now since the explosion which rocked to the Upper Big Branch Mine here in rural West Virginia. And as this community mourns the 25 who died, rescue teams are already preparing to go after the 4 who are still unaccounted for in the fading hope that they still make the alive.

Tonight, we are live to report on the tragedy in West Virginia where there's a race against time to reach 4 miners who may be still trapped at the end of a 7000 foot shaft into the mountain. And you'll hear for the first time from miners who made it out and survived the explosion. We drive across the mountain as community grieves. And you'll meet a woman who lost her husband, her two nephews, but her son barely escaped. Brian Ross investigates allegations of repeated safety violations by the company managing the mine. And we put tough questions to the chief executive as tonight we report on the miners who are in mourning, holding on, and questioning what happened to those they love. From ABC News, this is ABC World News with Diane Sawyer.

Good evening from West Virginia. we are live tonight because just down the road from here, it's the site of the worst mine disaster in this country in 26 years. And all night long, we have been talking to the people in these hills.

Words and Idioms

- desperate 필사적인
  - The prisoners grew increasingly **desperate**.
    죄수들은 갈수록 점점 더 될 대로 되라는 식이 되어 갔다.
  - She clung to the edge in a **desperate** attempt to save herself.
    그녀는 죽지 않기 위해 필사적으로 가장자리에 매달렸다.
- staggering death toll 깜짝 놀랄 희생자 수
  - He took the pills in **staggering** numbers.
    그는 엄청난 양의 알약을 복용했다.
  - The company is **staggering** under a ten-million debt.
    회사는 천만 달러의 빚으로 넘어져 가고 있다
- catastrophic 비극적인
  - He explains the Pew study's findings are hardly **catastrophic** or even that dramatic.
    그는 퓨 리서치 센터의 이번 여론 조사 결과는 비극적 결말이라거나 극적인 것은 아니라고 설명했습니다.
  - While **catastrophic** expenses are covered by insurance, day to day expenses are covered by the health savings account.
    막대한 비용은 보험으로 충당되는 반면 매일 지출되는 소소한 비용은 건강 예금 계좌에서 치러진다.
- herculean 엄청 힘든
  - Our **Herculean** efforts will some day ^come to fruition^.

우리의 초인적인 노력이 언젠가 결실을 맺고 말 겁니다.

- mineshaft 수직갱도
- Tonight, we are live to report on the tragedy in West Virginia where there's a **race against time** to reach 4 miners who may be still trapped at the end of a 7000 foot shaft into the mountain.
  - live [laiv]는 '생방송으로'라는 뜻이며, 장소를 나타내는 관계부사 where 는 앞에 있는 West Virginia를 수식한다. a race against time은 '시간과의 싸움'이라는 의미로 긴박한 상황에서 서두르는 모습을 나타낸다.
- And you'll meet a woman who lost her husband, her two nephews, but her son barely escaped.
  - who는 주격 관계대명사로 선행사 a woman 을 수식하는 제한적 용법으로 사용되었다. barely는 '겨우, 가까스로, 거의 ~ 않다'를 뜻하며 hardly 와 유사하다.

번역 웨스트버지니아 최대의 탄광사고

오늘 저녁 방송에서는 웨스트버지니아에서 발생한 탄광 재해 현장에서의 절망적인 시간과 놀랄 정도로 많은 사망자 수를 보도합니다. 현재, 탄광 회사의 안전 기록에 관한 새로운 질문이 제기되고 있습니다.
뉴욕의 NBC 뉴스 국제부에서 브라이언 윌리엄스 앵커가 진행하는 NBC Nightly News 입니다.

안녕하십니까, 지난 수년간 비극적인 사건이 꽤 많았던 웨스트버지니아의

석탄 탄광 업계에서 조차, 이번 일은 지하 깊은 곳에서 발생한 폭발 사건으로 인명 손실이 충격적입니다. 오늘 저녁, 광부 25명이 목숨을 잃었습니다. 다른 4명은 여전히 실종 상태입니다. 구조대원은 힘들지만 절박한 노력으로 탄광 내부에 갇힌 가스를 방출하기 위해 1,200피트 깊이로 구멍을 여러 개 뚫었습니다.

어제 충격적인 폭발로 어제 25명의 생명을 앗아간 빅 브랜치 광산의(사고) 근거지인 웨스트버지니아주 몽트콜에 나와있는 해리 스미스 기자입니다. 아직도 시체 18구가 지하 내부에 갇혔고, 광부 4명은 실종 상태입니다.
한편, 수직갱도 내부 공기는 유독 가스가 많습니다. 구조 작업이 불가능할 정도입니다. 따라서 가족과 친구 역시 희망과 절망 사이에 갇혀있습니다. 케이티 쿠릭이 진행하는 CBS 뉴스입니다. 오늘 저녁, 해리 스미스 기자가 웨스트버지니아에서 발생한 광산 재난 현장에서 보도합니다.

안녕하십니까, 케이티 앵커는 다른 임무를 맡고 있습니다. 웨스트버지니아 시골에 있는 이곳 어퍼 빅 브랜치 (Upper Big Branch) 탄광에서 요동친 폭발 사건이 발생한지 24시간이 넘었습니다. 또한, 이 지역사회가 사망자 25명을 애도하고 있을 때 구조팀들은 광부들이 아직도 살아있을 것이라는 희미한 희망 속에서 실종 상태의 광부 4명을 찾을 준비를 하고 있습니다.
오늘 저녁, 생방송으로 웨스트버지니아에서 발생한 비극적인 사건에 대해 보도합니다. 7,000피트되는 수직갱도 끝에 여전히 갇혔을지 모르는 광부 4을 찾기 위해 서두르고 있습니다. 또한, 폭발 현장을 빠져나와 생존한 광부들로부터 최초로 소식을 듣게 될 것입니다. 저희는 지역사회가 슬픔에 잠긴 이때 자동차로 산 일대를 둘러봤습니다. 그리고 남편과 두 사촌을 잃었지만 아들이 가까스로 탈출한 한 여성을 만날 것입니다. 브라이언 로스는 광산을 관리하는 회사의 반복된 안전 위반 사항에 대한 진술을 조사하고 있습니다. 그리고 슬픔을 참고 견디며, 자신들이 사랑하는 사람들에게 일어난 사건에 대해 의문을 던지고 있는 살아남은 광부들에 대해 보도합니다. 이때 저희는 기업 대표에게 난처한 질문을 던졌습니다. ABC 뉴스에서 다이앤 소여 앵커가 진행하는 ABC 월드 뉴스입니다.

웨스트버지니아에서 인사드립니다. 바로 여기 도로 아래 부분은 26년 만에 미국 내 최악의 광산 재해가 일어난 장소로 오늘 저녁 생방송으로 소식 전합니다. 밤새 저희는 이곳 언덕 지역에 거주하고 있는 사람들과 대화를 나눴습니다.

Dictation

- ____ ______ broadcast _________ tonight, desperate hours ____ ________ mine ________ ____ West Virginia
- ______ amid ______ staggering death toll,
- new questions now ________ ______ mining company's safety record.
- Nightly News begins now. _________ NBC News world headquarters ____ New York, ________ ____ NBC Nightly News ________ Brian Williams.
- Good evening. ____ ______ __ catastrophic explosion deep underground
- ______ ______ ________ ____ ________ ____ staggering, even ______ ______ coal mining industry ____ West Virginia
- ________ has seen ____ ________ tragedy over ______ ________.

- Tonight, 25 miners _____ _______. Another 4 _____ still missing.
- ___________ _ herculean _____ urgent effort under way _______ rescuers
- ____ drill several holes ____ deep ____ 1,200 feet down
- ____ release trapped gas inside _____ mine.
- ____'m Harry Smith ____ Montcoal, West Virginia, _______ ____ _____ Big Branch Mine
- _________ yesterday _ devastating explosion took _____ lives ____ 25 men.
- 18 bodies _____ still trapped inside _____ 4 miners _____ still unaccounted _____.
- _____ _____ air inside _____ mineshaft ____ ____ poisonous.
- Rescue work ____ impossible.
- ____ family _____ friends _____ trapped, too, between hope _____ despair.
- This ____ _____ CBS Evening News _______ Katie Couric, tonight Harry Smith reporting tonight ________ _____ site ____ _____ mine _______ ____ West Virginia.
- Good evening. Katie ____ ____ assignment.
- Well, ____ has _______ more _________ 24 hours now ________ _____ explosion

- which rocked ___ _____ Upper Big Branch Mine ________ ___ rural West Virginia.
- _____ ___ _______ community mourns _____ 25 _____ died,
- rescue teams _____ already preparing ___ go _________ _____ 4 _____ _____ still unaccounted _____
- ___ _____ fading hope _______ _______ still make _____ alive.
- Tonight, ___ _____ live ___ report ___ _____ tragedy ___ West Virginia
- _________ ____________ _ race _______ time ___ reach 4 miners
- _____ may _______ still trapped ___ _____ end ___ _ 7000 foot shaft _________ _____ mountain.
- _____ _________ hear _____ _____ _______ time ________ miners _____ _______ ___ _____ _____ survived _____ explosion.
- ___ drive across _____ mountain ___ community grieves.
- _____ _________ meet _ woman _____ lost her husband, her two nephews,
- _____ her son barely escaped.
- Brian Ross investigates allegations ___ repeated safety violations _______ _____ company managing _____ mine.
- _____ ___ put tough questions ___ _____ chief executive
- ___ tonight ___ report ___ _____ miners _____ _____ ___ mourning,

holding ____, ______ questioning ________ happened ____ _________ ________ love.

- _________ ABC News, ________ ____ ABC World News ________ Diane Sawyer.
- Good evening _________ West Virginia. ____ ______ live tonight because ________ down ______ road _________ _________, _______ ______ site ____ ______ worst mine ________
- ___ ________ ________ ____ 26 ________.
- ______ __________ night long, ____ _________ ________ talking ____ ______ ________ ____ these hills.

05

Trouble with Russian International adoptions

A day after the US and Russia agreed to a nuclear weapons treaty, relations are strained over a very different issue.

Russia's Foreign Minister called today for a ban on all adoptions by American families.

As Richard Roth reports, the move comes after a woman who adopted a Russian boy changed her mind and sent him back all by himself.

Russian authorities say the 7-year-old boy named Artyom arrived all alone in Moscow after an overnight flight from Washington with cookies and coloring pens in his backpack and a letter from his adoptive American mother.

I am sorry to say that for the safety of my family, friends, and myself , the letter said, I no longer wish to parent this child.

As he is a Russian national, I am returning him to your guardianship.

It was signed Torry Hansen.

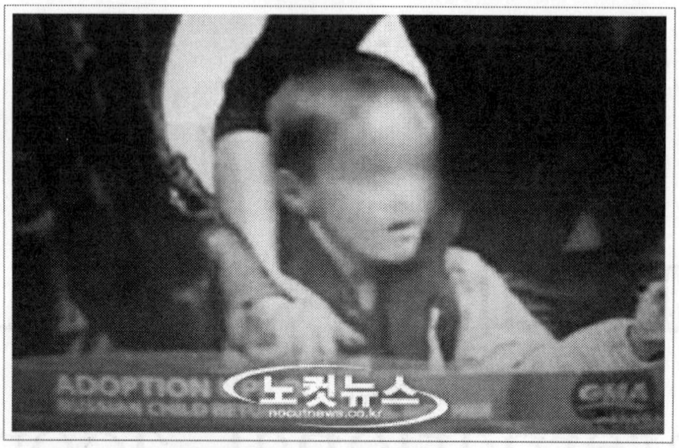

▲ 미국 가정에 입양됐다 버림받은 뒤 혼자 귀국한 러시아의 7세 소년 아르티옴 사벨리예프.(ABC-TV)

At a Siberian orphanage, they remember Hansen as the 33-year-old nurse from Tennessee who played happily with Artyom before adopting him last September.
But her letter called the boy violent and mentally unstable.
Shown on Russian TV today, talking to a child care official, Artyom's asked, "Did she hit you?"
"No" says the boy, gesturing to show his hair was pulled.
The Seattle agency that arranged the adoption tonight says it's saddened, but sheds no light on what happened.

The State Department says it's troubled by the case.
Tennessee authorities went to Torry Hansen's home looking for an explanation.
Her lawyer says she'll meet with them next week.
And in Moscow, officials say Artyom now needs good care, he needs to be rehabilitated.
“Did you cry?” he was asked. “Yes” he said.
“You're a man.” he was told, “You shouldn't.”
The 7-year-old is staying in Russia.

Richard Roth, CBS News, London.

Family shock. An American mother adopts a Russian boy, then sends the 7-year-old home alone.
Was he threatening? What would you do?
From ABC News, this is ABC World News with Diane Sawyer.
The Tennessee mother has returned the 7-year-old son she adopted from Russia sending him back alone.
And now outraged Russian officials want to halt adoptions to US families, period.

He arrived in Moscow Thursday alone and exhausted after flying half way around the world sparking international outrage .
He carried this note from his adopted mother back in Tennessee.
I adopted this child, wrote 32-year-old single mother Tory Hansen, he is violent and has severe psychopathic issues.
I was lied to and misled by the Russian Orphanage.
And after giving my best to this child, I'm sorry to say that for the safety of my family and myself, I no longer wish to parent this child.

Hansen adopted Artyom six months ago, but her family says the boy's hitting, kicking, spitting began to escalate.
He drew pictures of the family's house on fire.
Today, Russian President Dmitry Medvedec told ABC's George Stephanopoulos the incident is both illegal and immoral.
"It's monstrous on the part of the….of his adopted parents to take the kid and virtually throw him out."

Words and Idioms

- treaty 조약

  - The **treaty** was abrogated[annulled] by bilateral agreement.
    그 조약은 두 나라의 합의로 폐기되었다

- strained 긴장한

  - Her face looked **strained** and weary.
    그녀의 얼굴은 긴장한 것 같았고 지쳐 보였다.

- ban 금지

  - Chemical weapons are **banned** internationally.
    화학 무기는 국제적으로 금지되고 있다.

- adoptions 입양

  - The last ten years have seen a dramatic fall in the number of **adoptions**.
    지난 10년간 입양 건수는 극적으로 떨어졌다.

- national 국적

- guardianship 후견인

- orphanage 고아원

- unstable 불안정한

- arranged 중재하다

- sheds no light on 해결하다

- rehabilitated 재활치료

- outraged 화난

- halt 중지
- exhausted 기진맥진
- sparking 야기하다
- psychopathic 정신병적인
- misled 오도하다

번역 미-러시아 입양아 분규

미국과 러시아가 핵무기 조약을 체결한 다음 날, 양국 관계가 전혀 다른 이슈를 놓고 긴장 상태에 있습니다.
러시아 외무장관은 오늘 미국 가정으로의 모든 입양에 대해 금지하기로 했습니다.
리처드 로스 기자가 보도한 대로 러시아 남자 아이를 입양한 한 여성이 마음이 변해 남자 아이를 혼자 되돌려 보낸 사건이 있은 뒤 이 같은 움직임이 생겼습니다.

러시아 당국은 7살짜리 소년 아르티옴이 워싱턴에서 밤새 비행기를 타고 모스크바에 홀로 도착했다고 전했습니다. 아이 가방에는 쿠키와 색연필이 들어 있었고, 미국인 양모가 쓴 편지가 들어 있었습니다.
편지에는 "제 가족, 친구 및 저의 안전을 위해 그렇게 말하게 된 점은 유감입니다. 이 아이를 더 이상 양육하고 싶지 않습니다. 그 아이는 러시아인이니 후견인에게 돌려보내는 바입니다."라고 적혀 있었습니다. 토리 핸슨 씨가 서명한 편지였습니다.

한 시베리아 고아원 사람들은 한센 씨에 대해, 작년 9월 아르티옴을 입양하기 전 함께 행복하게 놀아주던 테네시주에서 온 33세 간호사로 기억하고 있습니다.

한편, 그녀의 편지에는 아이가 폭력적이고 정신적으로 불안정하다는 내용이 있었습니다.

오늘, 러시아 TV에 이 장면이 방영되었을 때 보육 담당자와의 대화에서 "그녀가 널 때렸니?"라는 질문을 받았습니다. 소년은 자신의 머리가 잡히는 모습을 몸짓으로 나타내면서 "아니에요"라고 답했습니다.

입양을 중재하는 시애틀 에이전시는 이번 일은 슬프지만 이번 사건에 대해 어떤 해명도 하지 않았습니다.

미 국무부는 이번 사건으로 곤경에 처했다고 전했습니다.

테네시주 당국은 자초지종을 듣기 위해 토리 핸슨씨 집으로 찾아갔습니다.

그녀의 담당 변호사에 따르면 핸슨씨가 다음 주 그들을 만날 예정이라고 합니다.

모스크바 관료들은 현재 아르티옴을 잘 보살펴야 하며 재활치료가 필요하다고 전했습니다.

"울었니?"라는 질문에 아이는 "네"라고 답했습니다.

아이는 "넌 남자야. 그러지 말아야지."라는 말을 들었습니다.

이 7살짜리 소년은 러시아에 머물고 있습니다.

런던에서 CBS 뉴스, 리처드 로스 기자였습니다.

입양 가정의 충격적인 소식입니다. 한 미국인 양모가 러시아 남자 아이를 입양한 후 7살짜리 아이를 홀로 고국으로 보냈습니다.

그 아이가 위협적이었나요? 여러분은 어떻게 했을까요?

ABC 뉴스에서 다이앤 소여 앵커가 진행하는 ABC월드 뉴스입니다 .

테네시주에 사는 양모는 러시아에서 입양한 7살짜리 아들을 홀로 되돌려 보냈습니다.

현재 분노한 러시아 관료들이 일정기간 미국 가정에 입양시키는 일을 중단하려고 합니다.
아이는 목요일, 모스크바에 홀로 도착했고 지구 반 바퀴를 비행한 뒤 기진맥진한 상태며, 이번 일은 국제적인 분쟁을 초래했습니다.
아이는 테네시주에 살고 있는 양모가 준 이 쪽지를 들고 왔습니다.
32살 싱글맘인 토리 한센 씨의 메모에는 "저는 이 아이를 입양했습니다. 아이가 난폭하며 심각한 정신적 문제가 있습니다. 저는 러시아 고아원 측에 속았습니다. 아이에게 최선을 다했지만 제 가족, 친구 및 저의 안전을 위해 그렇게 말하게 된 점은 유감입니다. 이 아이를 더 이상 양육하고 싶지 않습니다."라는 말이 적혀있었습니다.

한센 씨는 6개월 전 아르티옴을 입양했지만 그녀 가족에 의하면 소년은 때리기, 발차기, 침뱉기와 같은 행동이 점점 심해졌다고 합니다.
아이는 이 가족이 살고 있는 집이 불난 모습을 그렸습니다.
오늘, 드미트리 메드베데프 러시아 대통령은 ABC 방송의 조지 스테파노풀로스와의 대담에서 이번 사건은 불법적이고 부도덕한 일이라고 언급했습니다.
"입양부모가 아이를 데리고 간 뒤 사실상 아이를 버린 이번 일은 너무도 끔찍합니다."

Dictation

- ____ day ______ ______ US ______ Russia agreed ___ ___ nuclear weapons treaty , relations ______ strained __________ ____ _______ different issue.

- Russia's Foreign Minister called today ______ ____ ban ___ ____ adoptions

____ American families.

- ____ Richard Roth reports, _____ move comes _____ ____ woman _______ adopted ____ Russian boy changed _____ mind
- _____ sent _______ back ____ ____ himself.
- Russian authorities _____ _____ 7-year-old boy named Artyom arrived ____ alone ____ Moscow _____ ____ overnight flight _______ Washington
- _________ cookies _____ coloring pens ____ _____ backpack
- _____ ____ letter _______ _____ adoptive American mother.
- ____ am sorry ____ _____ _______ _____ _____ safety ____ ____ family, friends, _____ myself, _____ letter _______,
- ____ no longer wish ____ parent _______ child.
- ____ ____ ____ ____ Russian national, ____ am returning _______ ____ _____ guardianship.
- ____ _____ signed Torry Hansen.
- ____ ____ Siberian orphanage, _________ remember Hansen ____ _____ 33-year-old nurse _______ Tennessee
- _______ played happily ________ Artyom _______ adopting _______ _________ September.
- _____ _____ letter called _____ boy violent _____ mentally unstable .
- Shown ____ Russian TV today, talking ____ ____ child care official, Artyom's asked, "____ _____ _____ _______?"

- "No" _______ _____ boy, gesturing ___ show _____ hair _____ pulled.
- _____ Seattle agency _______ arranged _____ adoption tonight _______ _______ saddened, _____ sheds no light ___ _______ happened.
- _____ _____ Department _______ _______ troubled ___ _____ case.
- Tennessee authorities _________ ___ Torry Hansen's home looking _____ ___ explanation.
- _____ lawyer _______ _____'ll meet _________ _________ _________ week.
- _____ ___ Moscow , officials _____ Artyom now needs good care , ___ needs ___ _____ rehabilitated .
- "___ _______ cry?" ___ _____ asked. "Yes" ___ _______.
- "____________ ___ man." ___ _____ told, "_______ shouldn't."
- _____ 7-year-old ___ staying ___ Russia.
- Richard Roth, CBS News, London.
- Family shock. ___ American mother adopts ___ Russian boy, _______ sends _____ 7-year-old home alone.
- _____ ___ threatening? _______ _________ _______ do?
- _______ ABC News, _______ ___ ABC World News ________ Diane Sawyer.
- _____ Tennessee mother _____ returned _____ 7-year-old son _____ adoptcd _______ Russia scnding _______ back alone.

- _____ now outraged Russian officials want ____ halt adoptions ____ US families, period.
- ____ arrived ____ Moscow Thursday alone _____ exhausted ______ flying _______ way around _____ world sparking international outrage .
- ____ carried _______ note _______ _____ adopted mother back ____ Tennessee.
- ____ adopted _______ child, wrote 32-year-old single mother Tory Hansen,
- ____ ____ violent _____ _____ severe psychopathic issues.
- ____ _____ lied ____ _____ misled ____ _____ Russian Orphanage .
- _____ _____ giving ____ best ____ _______ child, ____'m sorry ____ _____
- _______ _____ _____ safety ____ ____ family _____ myself, ____ no longer wish ____ parent _______ child.
- Hansen adopted Artyom six months ago,
- _____ _____ family _______ _____ boy's hitting, kicking, spitting began ____ escalate.
- ____ drew pictures ____ _____ family's house ____ _____.
- Today, Russian President Dmitry Medvedec told ABC's George Stephanopoulos _____ incident ____ both illegal _____ immoral.
- "_______ monstrous ____ _____ part ____ _____….____ _____ adopted parents ____ _______ _____ kid _____ virtually . throw _______ _____."

06

Increasing that American teens are texting

And letting their fingers do the talking.

Many teens are now texting more than a hundred times a day.

From CBS News world headquarters in New York, this is the CBS Evening News.

And finally tonight, the number of American teenagers who text has skyrocketed over the past few years.

It's hard to believe that a new study says nearly one in three kids over the age of 12 sends more than one hundred texts a day.

Ben Tracey has more now on these teen text addicts.

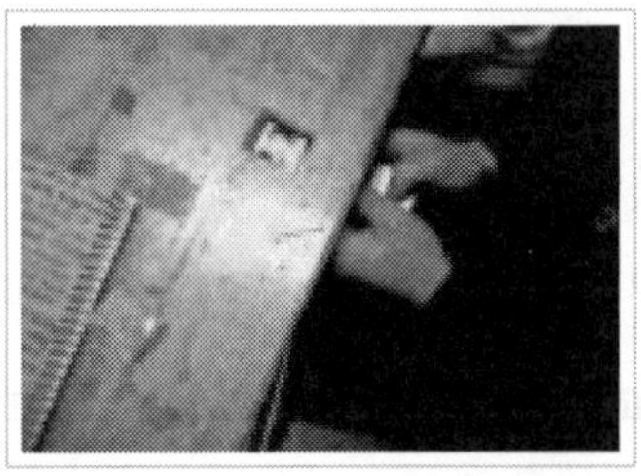

At school these days, the cell phone is now as common as the backpack.

“Do you know of anyone who doesn't have a cell phone?” “Actually no!”
In fact, four of five teens admit to sleeping with having their cell phone near their bed.
“When you go to sleep at night, where is your cell phone?”
“My cell phone is right beside me.” “In your bed?” “Yes, sir.”
At Fairfax High School in Los Angeles, phones are banned in the classroom.
But lunchtime is a cellular feeding frenzy.

Most students banging out text after text after text.
“How have you been?” “What are you doing today?” “How was your weekend? Normal stuff.”
The average adult sends just 10 text messages per day, but older teenage girls send about 3,000 per month.
16-year-old Annie Levitz sent about 4,000 per month.
She now has carpal tunnel syndrome and needs surgery.
Social studies teacher Mike Stryer says some of his students admit they're hooked.
"I mean they actually say that we are addicted to texting and it's interfering with their studies and their lives. "

Texting is now the main way teens communicate with their friends.
So some parents are concerned that their kids no longer sit down and simply have conversations.
"We don't get the nonverbal training that we need for later in life, on a job interview, talking with our friends, consoling friends. We're missing that along the way."
But to teens glued to their phones, that's one message that apparently isn't getting through.
Ben Tracey, CBS News, Los Angeles.

Words and Idioms

- feeding frenzy 무자비한 사용 / 먹잇감에 달려드는 광란 상태
  - The reporter was in a **feeding frenzy.**
    기자는 특종을 찾아다니는 열광정적이 상태에 있었다.
  - That's a lot to stay on top of when you're in the middle of a **feeding frenzy** for the most marketable commodity in music.
    가장 인기 있는 그룹이 되기 위해 치열한 경쟁을 벌이는 세계 대중음악계에서 최고의 자리를 지킨다는 것은 정말 엄청난 일이다.
- banging out 단숨에 쓰다 /(기사 등을)워드로 치다.
  - It was surprising how he could **bang out** an essay.
    그가 에세이를 단숨에 쓸 수 있어서 놀라웠다.
  - I got a **bang out** of it.
    그거에 흥분됐었어요.
- carpal tunnel syndrome 팔목 터널 증후군
  - The disorders include **carpal tunnel syndrome**, back pain, and tendinitis.
    척추에 영향을 미치는 질환으로 팔목압박증후군이나 요통 혹은 건염이 이에 속합니다.
- nonverbal 말이 서투른/비언어적인
  - Gestures are **nonverbal** behaviors that translate words or phrases rather directly.
    제스처라는 것은 말로 하지 않고 단어나 구를 다소 직접적으로 표현하는 행동입니다.
- consoling 위로하다
  - It is **consoling[comforting]** that nobody was killed in the accident.
    그 사고에 사망자가 없었다는 것은 불행 중 다행이다.

- In fact, four or five teens admit to sleeping with having their cell phone near their bed.

  * [admit to(전치사) + 명사 / 동명사]는 ~을 시인(인정)하다는 의미다.

    Ex) She admitted to having stolen the handbag

    그녀는 그 핸드백을 훔쳤다고 자백했다.

- In fact, four or five teens admit to sleeping with having their cell But to teens glued to their phones, that's one message that apparently isn't getting through.

  * glue는 '접착제로 붙이다. ~에 집중하다'로 여기서는 휴대폰에서 떨어지지 않는 십대들을 나타내는데 쓰였다. get through는 '생각을 이해시키다. 이해되다'는 의미이다.

번역 미 십대 문자 보내기 급증

손가락으로 이야기합니다.

수많은 청소년들이 하루에 일백 번 이상 문자메시지를 주고받습니다.

뉴욕 CBS 뉴스 국세부에서 CBS 이브닝 뉴스 전해드립니다.

오늘 저녁, 마지막 소식입니다. 문자메시지를 보내는 미국 십대들의 수가 지난 수년간 급등했습니다.

새로운 연구에 따르면 12살이 넘는 청소년 3 명 중 1 명은 하루 100건 이상의 문자메시지를 보낸다고 하는데요, 믿기 힘든 내용입니다.

벤 트레이시 기자가 지금부터 문자 중독에 빠진 청소년에 관한 소식을 상세히 보도합니다.

요즘 학교에서 휴대폰은 가방만큼이나 흔합니다.

"휴대폰을 가지고 있지 않은 학생이 있나요", "실제적으로 없습니다!"

사실, 4-5 명의 청소년들이 침대 근처에 휴대폰을 두고 잠을 잔다고 했습니다.
"저녁에 잠자리에 들 때 핸드폰을 어디에 두나요?"
"제 옆에 둡니다.", "침대 말이죠?", "네 ,그렇습니다."
로스앤젤레스의 페어팩스 고등학교는 교실 내 휴대폰 사용을 금지하고 있습니다.
하지만 점심시간이 되면 (학생들은) 휴대폰을 무지막지하게 사용합니다.

학생들 대부분은 문자메시지를 보내고 또 보내고, 단숨에 메시지를 써 내려갑니다.
"어떻게 지내?", "오늘 뭐할 거니?", "주말 어땠어? 등 평범한 내용이죠."
보통의 어른은 하루에 문자를 10건 정도 보냅니다.
한편, 좀 더 나이든 십대 소녀들은 문자메시지를 한 달 3,000 통 가량 보냅니다.
16세인 애니 레비츠는 매달 4,000 여 건의 문자메시지를 보냅니다.
그녀는 현재 팔목 터널 증후군을 앓고 있고 외과 수술이 필요합니다.
사회 교사인 마이크 스트라이어는 담당 학생 중 일부가 중독됐다고 했습니다.
"제 말은 학생들이 사실상 자신들이 문자메시지에 중독됐다고 말했습니다.
이는 학생들의 학습과 생활을 방해합니다."

문자는 십대들이 친구들과 소통하는 주요 방식입니다.
이에 따라 몇몇 부모님들은 자녀들이 더 이상 앉아서 대화하지 않는 사실에 염려합니다.
"친구와 대화하고 친구를 위로하면서 훗날 면접에서 필요한 언어적인 훈련을 받지 못합니다. 그런 와중에 놓치게 되는 겁니다."
하지만 휴대폰에 눈을 떼지 못하는 십대들에게는 분명 이해가 안 되는 메시지입니다.
로스앤젤레스에서 CBS 뉴스, 벤 트레이시 기자였습니다.

Dictation

- ______ letting ________ fingers do ______ talking.
- Many teens ______ now texting more __________ ___ hundred times ___ day.
- ________ CBS News world headquarters ___ New York, ________ ___ ______ CBS Evening News.
- ______ finally tonight, ______ number ___ American teenagers ________ ________ ______ skyrocketed ________ ______ _____ few ________.
- ______ hard ___ __________ ________ ___ new study says nearly one ___ three kids ________ ______ age ___ 12
- sends more __________ one hundred texts ___ day.
- Ben Tracey ______ more now ___ __________ teen ________ addicts.
- ___ school __________ days, ______ cell phone ___ now ____ common ____ ______ backpack.
- "Do ______ ______ ___ anyone ________ doesn't ________ ___ cell phone ?" "Actually no!"
- ___ ________, __________ of five teens admit ___ sleeping ________ having ________ cell phone near ________ bed.
- "________ ______ go ___ sleep ___ night, __________ ___ ________ cell phone?"

- “___ cell phone ___ right beside _____.” “___ _______ bed?” “Yes, sir.”
- ___ Fairfax High School ___ Los Angeles, phones _____ banned ___ _____ classroom.
- _____ lunchtime ___ ___ cellular feeding frenzy .
- _______ students banging _____ _______ _______ _______ _______ _______.
- “How _______ _____ _______? ”, “ _______ _____ _____ doing today?”, “How _____ _______ weekend? Normal stuff.”
- _____ average adult sends _______ 10 _______ messages per day,
- _____ older teenage girls send _____ 3,000 per month.
- 16 -_________-old Annie Levitz sent _____ 4,000 per month.
- _____ now _____ carpal tunnel syndrome _____ needs surgery.
- Social studies teacher Mike Stryer says some ___ _______ students admit _________'re hooked.
- "___ mean _________ actually _____ _______ ___ _____ addicted ___ texting _____ _____ interfering _______ _______ studies _____ _______ lives."
- Texting ___ now _____ main way teens communicate _______ _______ friends.
- So some parents _____ concerned _______ _______ kids no longer sit down _____ simply _______ conversation s .

- " ___ _________ get _____ nonverbal training _______ ___ need _____ _________ ___ life, ___ ___ job interview,
- talking _______ _______ friend s , consoling friends . _______ missing _______ along _____ way."
- _____ ___ teens glued ___ _______ phones, _______'s one message _______ apparently isn't getting through.
- Ben Tracey, CBS News, Los Angeles.

07

Guard against aliens

Steven Hawking is in the news tonight.

As one of the bona fide smart people on the planet when the renowned astrophysicist warned us about aliens from outer space this weekend, people tended to listen up.

On his new discovery network series, Steven Hawking says if aliens visit us here on earth, "The outcome would be much as when Columbus landed in America which didn't turn out well for the Native Americans," end of quote.

Make a note, he indicates we should stay away from them at all costs.

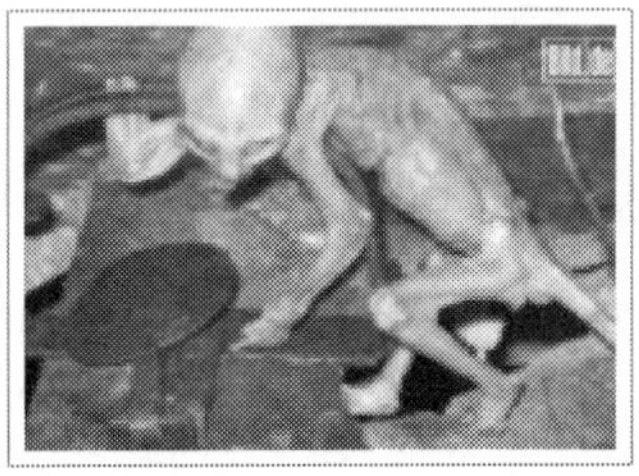

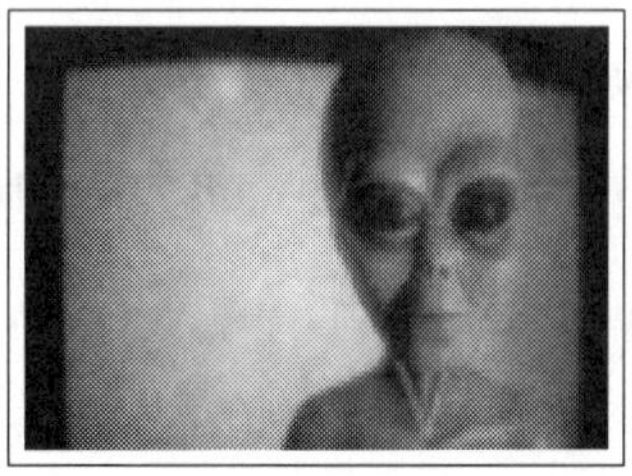

And outer space. The most admired scientist in the world says aliens do exist and don't be so sure if they are friends.

From ABC News, this is ABC World News with Diane Sawyer.

Finally tonight, maybe no one on planet earth has a keener grasp of the cosmos than Steven Hawking.
So when the renowned astrophysicist warns of the risk posed by aliens, what is he talking about? Nick Watt on what Hawking has to say.

We are a species obsessed with the question.
What else, who else is out there?
From the War of the worlds to Independence Day, we've imagined alien invasion.
Now Steven Hawking says theoretically this could happen.
"To my mathematical brain, the numbers alone make thinking about aliens perfectly rational."
100 billion galaxies out there, why would earth be the only populated planet?
"When the smartest man in the world utters anything, it's an occasion to listen, even if it's a little bit humorous."
"You would be inexcusably egocentric to suggest that life on earth is alone in the universe."

He doesn't think they'll all be like Alien 2. But any alien that makes its earth could be unfriendly.
"The outcome would be much as when Christopher Columbus first landed in America which didn't turn out very well for the Native Americans."
I've spent some time with UFO believers and I thought they were just lunatics.
"I don't like photographs. I don't like the flash.", "All right."
Looks like I'm the chump.
Hawking believes aliens in huge spaceships might really be searching for planets to colonize.

Hang on! Was Dr. Martin and killers from space right all along?

"Where did you come from?"

"From a planet yet unknown to you!"

Nick Watt, ABC News, London.

Words and Idioms

- bona fide 진짜로
- astrophysicist 천체물리학자
- keener grasp 간절한 이해
- species 종
- obsessed 사로잡혀있는 / 사로잡다
- utters 말하다
- inexcusably egocentric 용납할 수 없이 자기중심적인
- lunatics 미치광이 / 정신이상의
- chump 얼간이 / 속이다
- "The outcome would be **much as** when Columbus landed in America which didn't turn out well for the Native Americans," end of quote.

  * **much as**는 '~와 같은 정도로'의 뜻으로, 콜럼버스가 아메리카 대륙

을 발견할 당시 거주하고 있던 원주민들에게 해를 끼쳤던 상황과 유사할 것이라는 내용이다. turn out well은 '번영하다, 잘 풀리다'는 의미이다.

- Hawking believes aliens in huge spaceships might really be **searching for** planets to colonize.

  * **search for**(~을 찾다)는 추측을 나타내는 조동사 might와 진행형(be+ -ing)를 써서 지금도 무언가를 찾고 있을 것이다 라는 내용을 표현했다. to colonize(식민지로 개척하다)는 to 부정사의 형용사적 용법으로 planet 을 수식한다.

번역 외계인을 경계하라

스티븐 호킹 박사가 오늘 저녁 뉴스에 등장합니다.
지구상에서 진정으로 명석한 사람 중 한 하나로 이 저명한 천체 물리학자가 이번 주말 우주 공간의 외계인에 대해 경고하자 사람들이 귀를 기울였습니다.
새로운 디스커버리 채널 시리즈에서 스티브 호킹 박사가 만일 외계인이 이곳 지구의 인간을 찾아온다면 "콜럼버스가 미국에 상륙하자 원주민들에게 좋지 못한 일이 생긴 것과 같은 결과가 생길 것이다"고 말미에 덧붙였습니다.
유념해 두시기 바랍니다. 호킹 박사는 인간이 어떻게 해서든 외계인과의 접촉을 피해야 한다고 언급했습니다.

우주 관련 소식입니다. 세상에서 가장 존경받는 과학자가 외계인이 존재하며, 그들이 우호적인 존재일지 너무 확신하지 말라고 했습니다.
ABC 뉴스에서 다이앤 소여 앵커가 진행하는 ABC 월드 뉴스입니다.
오늘 마지막 소식입니다. 지구상에서 스티븐 호킹 박사보다 혜성에 대해 더 예리한 통찰력을 지닌 사람은 아무도 없을 것입니다.
저명한 천체 물리학자가 외계 생명체로 인해 야기될 위험성을 경고할 때, 그는 무엇을 이야기한 것일까요?
닉 와트 기자가 호킹 박사가 전하려는 바를 보도합니다.

인간은 "저 우주에는 무엇이, 누가 있을까?라는 질문에 사로잡혀 있는 종(種) 입니다.
영화〈우주전쟁: The War of the worlds〉에서 〈인디펜던스 데이 : Independence Day〉에 이르기까지 우리는 외계인의 침략을 상상했습니다.
스티븐 호킹 박사에 따르면 이론상 이 같은 일이 발생할 수 있다고 합니다.
수학적인 두뇌로 수치 자체만 놓고 볼 때 외계인에 관한 생각은 완벽히 합리적이다."
우주에는 1천억 개의 은하가 존재하는데 왜 지구에만 사람이 살겠습니까?
"세계에서 가장 똑똑한 사람이 무언가를 말하면 그 내용이 약간 웃기더라도 듣게 됩니다."
"우주에서 지구에만 생명체가 존재한다고 한다면 당신은 용납할 수 없을 만큼 자기중심적인 사람일 겁니다."

그는 외계인이 모두 영화 〈에일리언 2〉와 같을 거라고 생각하지 않습니다.
하지만 영토를 만드는 외계인이라면 우호적이지 않을 수도 있습니다.
"콜럼버스가 미국에 상륙하자 원주민들에게 좋지 못한 일이 생긴 것과 같은 결과가 생길 것이다."
저는 얼마간 UFO 신봉자들과 시간을 보내면서 이들이 괴짜라고 생각했습니다.
"전 사진을 좋아하지 않습니다. 플래시도 싫고요.", "그렇군요."
제가 바보처럼 보이는군요.
호킹 박사는 거대한 우주선을 탄 외계인들이 정말로 식민지화할 행성을 찾고 있을지도 모른다고 생각합니다.

잠깐! 마틴 박사와 우주에서 온 킬러들이 옳았다는 거야?
"어디에서 왔지?"
"미지의 행성에서"
런던에서 ABC 뉴스, 닉 와트 기자였습니다.

Dictation

- Steven Hawking ___ ___ _____ news tonight.
- ___ one __ _____ bona fide smart _______ __ _____ planet _______ _____ renowned astrophysicist warned us
- _____ aliens _______ outer space _______ weekend, _______ tended __ listen __.
- __ _______ new discovery network series,
- Steven Hawking says _______ aliens visit us _____ __ earth,
- "_____ outcome _______ __ much __ _______ Columbus landed __ America
- which _______ turn _____ well _____ _____ Native Americans," end __ quote.
- _______ __ note, he indicates __ _______ stay away _______ _________ __ all costs.
- _____ outer space. _____ _______ admired scientist __ _____ world

says aliens do exist

- ______ __________ ___ so sure ________ __________ ______ friends.
- ________ ABC News, ________ ___ ABC World News ________ Diane Sawyer.
- Finally tonight, maybe no one ___ planet earth ______ ___ keener grasp ___ ______ cosmos __________ Steven Hawking.
- So ________ ______ renowned astrophysicist warns ___ ______ risk posed ___ aliens,
- ________ ___ he talking ______? Nick Watt ___ ________ Hawking ______ ___ ______.
- ___ ______ ___ species obsessed ________ ______ question.
- ________ else, ________ else ___ ______ __________?
- ________ ______ War ___ ______ worlds ___ Independence Day, ______ imagined alien invasion.
- Now Steven Hawking says theoretically ________ ________ happen.
- "___ ___ mathematical brain, ______ numbers alone ________ thinking ______ aliens perfectly rational."
- 100 billion galaxies ______ __________, __________ ________ earth ___ ______ only populated planet?
- "________ ______ smartest man ___ ______ world utters anything,
- ______ ___ occasion ___ listen, even ________ ______ ___ little bit

humorous."

- "_____ _______ ___ inexcusably egocentric ___ suggest
- _______ life ___ earth ___ alone ___ _____ universe."
- He doesn't think ________'ll all ___ _____ Alien 2. _____ any alien _______ makes its earth _______ ___ unfriendly.
- "_____ outcome _______ ___ much ___ _______ Christopher Columbus _______ landed ___ America
- which _______ turn _____ very well _____ _____ Native Americans."
- _____ spent some time _______ UFO believers _____ ___ thought ________ _______ _______ lunatics .
- "___ _________ _____ photographs. ___ _________ _____ _____ flash." "All right."
- Looks _____ _____ _____ chump .
- Hawking believes aliens ___ huge spaceships might really ___ searching _____ planets ___ colonize.
- Hang ___! _____ Dr. Martin _____ killers _______ space right all along?
- "________ _____ _____ come _______?"
- "_______ ___ planet yet unknown ___ _____!"
- Nick Watt, ABC News, London.

08

Economic Crisis of Greece and Memory of Vietnam war

Turning now to Greece where the public backlash sparked by the country's debt crisis turned deadly today.

Protestors are furious about massive spending cuts and tax increases.

They were supposed to save that country from bankruptcy.

Now fears are growing that the bailout in Greece won't work.

That could cause ripple effects across Europe and here in the United States.

Our report tonight from NBC's Dawna Friesen.

They came in their tens of thousands flooding the streets of central Athens.

“Only the people pay and the politicians do nothing!”
They tried to storm the Greek parliament. Tear gas forced them back.
As riot police fought running battles, smoke drifted over the acropolis from firebombed building and vehicles.

Inside this bank, 17 employees managed to escape, but three including a pregnant woman were overcome by smoke.
The deaths have sparked shock and outrage.
A demonstration is one thing, said the Greek prime minister, murder is quite another.

All this chaos is because Greeks are furious at austerity measures imposed on them as part of a $141 billion bailout package.
The International Monetary Fund and European countries will hand over the cash, but only if Greece makes massive cuts to public salaries and pensions and increases taxes.
For a gcncration known for its lavish spending and tax avoidance, it's all a step too far.
The fear is that if Greece can't get its financial act together, then other countries with huge debts like Spain, Portugal and Ireland could be next, could need bailouts, too, which might trigger another European, possibly global financial crisis.

“The debt is rising very, very rapidly. They have little prospect of economic growth.
So if you look ahead a few years, not where we are now, if something doesn't

change, they could also be in very serious trouble."

The pain is confined to Greece for now, but investors the world over are jittery wondering if the debt crisis will spread.

Dawna Friesen, NBC news, London.

Today marks an anniversary more than one American generation won't forget.

Here is how John Chancello described the end of the Vietnam War on this broadcast 35 years ago tonight.

"Good evening. The city of Saigon was renamed today.

The victorious communist who forced the city surrender said the capital of South Vietnam, henceforth, will be known as Ho Chi Minh City."

That word came as North Vietnamese forces overran the city captured the presidential palace while the last Americans fled in a chaotic evacuation from the US embassy.

US combat role had ended two years earlier.

More than 58,000 Americans and a million Vietnamese died in that war.

Words and Idioms

- backlash (사회 변화에 대한 민중들의 반발)
  - The government is facing an angry **backlash** from voters over the new tax.
    그 새로 생긴 세금 때문에 정부가 유권자들의 심한 반발에 직면해 있다.

• furious 화난

- She was absolutely **furious** at having been deceived.
  그녀는 그동안 속아 온 것에 대해 그야말로 길길이 뛰었다.

• bailout 구제금융

- On 25 Oct 2008 the Financial Times reports that Iceland applied to the IMF for a **bailout**.
  2008년 10월 25일 Financial Times지가 보도하기를 아이슬랜드가 IMF에 구제금융을 신청했다고 한다.

• ripple effects 파급효과

- His resignation will have a **ripple effect** on the whole department.
  그의 사직은 부서 전체에 파급 효과가 있을 것이다.

• acropolis 그리스의 성채

- The Parthenon is on a big hill in Athens called the **Acropolis**.
  파르테논은 아크로폴리스라고 불리는 아테네의 큰 언덕에 있다.

• austerity measures 긴축조치

- But it would fit the new mood of national **austerity**.
  하지만, 그 것은 새로운 국가 긴축 분위기에 적절하다.

• lavish 풍성한

- She **lavishes** most of her attention on her youngest son.
  그녀는 지나칠 정도로 관심의 대부분을 막내아들에게 쏟는다.

• jittery 초초한

- It's my first time, and I'm just **jittery** about the whole thing.
  난 처음이라서 모든 게 불안해.

• henceforth 지금부터/ 그 이후로

- Friday 31 July 1925 **henceforth** became known as 'Red Friday'.
  1925년 7월 31일 금요일은 그 이후로 '피의 금요일'로 알려지게 되었다.

– A demonstration is **one thing**, said the Greek prime minister, murder is quite **another**.

* one thing~another…: ~ 와 …는 별개이다 (다르다).

– The pain **is confined to** Greece for now, but investors the world over are jittery.

* confine(한정하다, 제한하다)가 전치사 to와 함께 쓰여 **be confined to**는 '~에 제한되어 있다, 갇혀있다'는 뜻이 된다.

– They have **little** prospect of economic growth.

* 여기에서 little(거의 없는)은 셀 수 없는 명사를 수식한다. 한편 , 셀 수 있는 명사 앞에는 few를 써 준다.

번역 그리스 경제 위기와 베트남 전쟁 기억

국가 부채 위기가 발단이 되어 오늘, 대중들의 반발이 빗발치고 있는 그리스 소식을 전해 드리겠습니다.
시위대는 막대한 경비 삭감과 세금 인상에 분노했습니다.
이들은 은행 파산으로부터 국가를 구제해야 했습니다.
현재, 그리스의 긴급구조금융이 효과를 발휘하지 못할 것이라는 두려움이 일고 있습니다.
이번 사건은 유럽 전역과 이곳 미국에 파급효과를 줄 수 있습니다.
NBC 뉴스의 도나 프리센 기자가 보도합니다.

수만 명이 아테네 거리를 가득 메웠습니다.
"시민들만 세금을 내고 정치인들은 아무 일도 하지 않습니다!"
이들은 그리스 국회를 습격하려고 했습니다. 그러자 경찰은 최루 가스를 발사했습니다.

진압 경찰들이 추격전을 벌일 때 소이탄 공격을 받은 빌딩과 차량의 연기가 아크로폴리스 너머를 떠 다녔습니다.

이 은행 건물내부에서 직원 17명은 가까스로 빠져 나왔지만 임산부를 포함한 3명은 연기로 질식했습니다.

이 죽음은 충격과 분노를 불러 일으켰습니다.

그리스 수상은 '시위와 살인은 별개'라고 밝혔습니다.

이 모든 혼란은 그리스인들이 1,410억 달러 규모의 긴급구제금융의 일부로 시민들에게 부과된 긴축조치에 분노했기 때문입니다.

IMF(국제통화기금)와 유럽 국가들이 자금은 빌려줄 예정이지만 시민의 봉급 및 연금에 대해 그리스는 막대한 긴축 정책을 펼치고 세금을 올릴 경우에 한해서입니다.

풍부한 지출과 과세 회피로 잘 알려진 세대에게는 모든 것이 너무도 지나친 조치입니다.

우려되는 사항은 그리스가 서로 재정적인 조치를 협력하여 해결하지 못할 경우 스페인, 포르투갈 및 아일랜드 등 엄청난 부채를 안고 있는 다른 국가 또한 그 다음 차례가 될 수 있고, 긴급구제금융이 필요할 수 있다는 점입니다.

"부채는 대단히 빠르게 늘어나고 있습니다. 그들은 경제 성장에 대해 기대가 거의 없습니다.

향후 몇 년을 전망하자면 우리가 있는 현재 상황은 아닐 것입니다.

무엇인가 변하지 않는다면 그들 역시 매우 심각한 상황에 처할 수 있습니다.

그 고통은 현재로선 그리스에 국한되어 있지만, 전 세계 투자자들은 부채 위기가 확산될지 여부를 궁금해 하며 초조해 합니다.

런던에서 NBC 뉴스, 도나 프리센 기자였습니다.

오늘은 미국의 한 세대 이상 잊지 못할 기념일을 나타냅니다.

존 챈셀로 기자가 35년 전 바로 오늘 저녁 본 방송에서 보도된 베트남 전쟁 종식을 어떻게 설명했는지를 보여줍니다.
“안녕하십니까, 사이공 시가 오늘 새로운 이름을 갖게 됐습니다.
도시를 항복시킨 승리한 공산당원은 남 베트남의 수도가 지금부터 호치민 시로 알려질 것이라고 했습니다.
그 표현은 도시를 함락시킨 북부 베트남군이 대통령 궁을 점령했을 때 나온 말입니다.
한편, 마지막 미국인들은 미 대사관에서 우왕좌왕하며 대피했습니다.
미 전투 임무는 2년 앞서 종식됐습니다.
이 전쟁에서 5만 8천 명의 미국인과 수백만 명의 베트남 국민들이 사망했습니다.

Dictation

- Turning now ___ Greece _________ ______ public backlash sparked ___ ______ country's _______ crisis turned deadly today.
- Protestors ______ furious about _________ spending ________ ______ tax increases.
- _______ _______ supposed ___ _____ ________ country _______ bankruptcy.
- Now fears ______ growing ________ ______ bailout ___ Greece _____ work.
- ________ _______ cause ripple effects across Europe ______ _______ ___ ______ United States.

• Our report tonight ______ NBC's Dawna Friesen.

• ______ ______ __ ______ ______ __ thousands flooding _____ streets __ central Athens.

• "______ _____ people _____ _____ _____ politicians do nothing!"

• ______ tried __ ______ _____ Greek parliament. ______ ______ forced ______ back.

• __ riot police fought running battles,

• ______ drifted ______ _____ acropolis ______ firebombed building _____ vehicles.

• Inside _______ bank, 17 employees managed __ escape,

• _____ three including __ pregnant woman ______ ________ __ ______.

• _____ deaths ______ sparked shock _____ outrage.

• __ demonstration __ one ______, ______ _____ Greek prime minister, ______ __ _______ another.

• All _______ _______ __ because Greeks _____ furious __ austerity measures imposed ____ ______

• __ _______ __ __ $141 billion bailout package.

• _____ International Monetary Fund _____ European countries ______ ______ ______ _____ _______,

• _____ ______ ___ Greece _______ ________ _______ __ public salaries _____ pensions _____ increases taxes.

- _____ ___ generation known _____ _______ lavish spending _____ tax avoidance, it's all ___ step too far.
- _____ fear ___ _______ ____ Greece can't get _______ financial act together,
- then other countries with huge debts like Spain, Portugal _____ Ireland
- ______ ____ next, ______ need bailouts, too,
- which might trigger another European, possibly global financial crisis.
- "_____ ______ ___ rising very, very rapidly. ______ ______ little prospect ___ economic growth.
- So ____ you look ahead ___ few years, not ________ ____ _____ now,
- ____ something doesn't change, ______ ______ also ____ ___ very serious trouble."
- _____ pain ___ confined ___ Greece _____ now, _____ investors _____ world ______ _____ jittery
- wondering ___ _____ ______ crisis ______ spread.
- Dawna Friesen, NBC news, London.
- Today marks ___ anniversary more than one American generation ____ forget.
- ______ ___ how John Chancello described _____ ______ ___ _____ Vietnam War ____ _______ broadcast 35 years ago tonight.
- "Good evening. _____ city ___ Saigon was renamed today.

- _____ victorious communist who forced _____ city surrender ______ _____ capital __ South Vietnam, henceforth , ______ _____ known __ Ho Chi Minh City."

- _______ word ______ __ North Vietnamese forces overran _____ city captured _____ presidential palace

- ______ _____ _____ Americans fled __ __ chaotic evacuation ______ _____ US embassy.

- US combat ______ ______ ______ two years earlier.

- More than 58,000 Americans _____ __ million Vietnamese ______ __ _______ war.

09

Save Monarch Butterfly

And that they are insect royalty.

But now their kingdom is under attack.

We end tonight with one of nature's most beautiful creatures and greatest mysteries.

No one knows why, but every fall, nearly every Monarch Butterfly in North America migrates to central Mexico.

But now as Seth Doane tells us, the Monarchs went to resort is going through its own metamorphosis.

Every spring, these blue skies turn orange.

For centuries, millions of Monarch butterflies have come to these same ancient forests, traveling from as far away as Maine, North Dakota, even Canada.

They weigh just a fifth of a penny, but so many flapping wings can sound like falling rain.

For veteran conservationist, Bill Toone, this site is both awesome and troubling.
There are an estimated 250 million Monarch butterflies that winter in this preserve.
That sounds like a lot, it certainly looks like a lot, but imagine 15 years ago, there were nearly one billion.
The problem is these giant fir trees where Monarchs huddle for warmth are being cut down.
This was the forest next to the butterfly grounds in 2004.
By 2008, it looked like this.

Without cover, millions of butterflies can freeze to death.
In an average year, up to 15 %.
This year, bad weather killed more than 50 %.
The Mexican government set aside about 140,000 acres as a protected zone for the Monarch Butterflies.
Still, inside this zone, every year, more than 100,000 trees are cut down.

Mexico recently lost nearly 7% of its forests, an area twice the size of New Jersey, much of it from illegal logging.
Deforestation threatens more than Monarchs.
It destroys watersheds which can cause mudslides.
This one, five miles from the butterfly sanctuary killed 17 people.
But even average families contribute to the problem, consuming about 40 trees a

year to cook and heat their homes.

Now, Monarchs are leaving these forests, mating along the way.
Over summer, four generations will be born and die, each living about a month before a super generation arrives.
They'll live seven months, and having never been to Mexico before.
Saving the migration means saving the forest.
The question is, how much time do these Monarchs really have?
Seth Doane, CBS News, Michoacan, Mexico.

Words and Idioms

- metamorphosis 변형 변태
  - She had undergone an amazing **metamorphosis** from awkward schoolgirl to beautiful woman.
    그녀는 볼품없던 여학생에서 아름다운 여인으로 놀랍게 탈바꿈해 있었다.
- fir trees 전나무
- watersheds 분수계
  - The middle decades of the 19th century marked a **watershed** in Russia's history.
    19세기 중반 몇 십 년은 러시아 역사에 있어 중요한 분수령이 되었다.
  - so many **flapping** wings can sound like falling rain.
    * **flap**(날갯짓 하다, 퍼덕 거리다)은 '날갯짓을 히는'과 같이 능동의

의미를 나타내기 위해 현재분사 **flapping**을 써 준다. sound like(~처럼 들리다)에서 like는 전치사이므로 뒤에 나오는 단어의 형태는 명사 / 동명사가 된다.

- For veteran conservationist, Bill Toone, this site is **both** awesome **and** troubling.

  * veteran conservationist 와 Bill Toone은 동격으로 쓰였다. 상관접속사인 [both A and B]는 'A, B 둘 다 모두'이며 이에 대응하여 [neither A nor B]는 'A도 B도 아닌'이 있다.

번역 호랑나비를 구하자

호랑나비는 왕족 곤충입니다.

그러나 이들의 왕국이 공격받고 있습니다.

자연에서 가장 아름다운 생명체이자 가장 신비로운 존재 중 하나로 오늘 뉴스를 마감하겠습니다.

해마다 가을이면 북미의 대부분의 호랑나비들이 중앙 멕시고 지역으로 왜 이동하는지 이유를 아는 사람은 없습니다.

지금부터 셋 돈 기자가 보도할 내용처럼 철따라 이동한 호랑나비가 변형 과정을 겪고 있다고 합니다.

매해 봄이 되면 이 푸른 하늘은 오렌지 빛으로 바뀝니다.

수 세기 동안, 수백만 마리의 호랑나비들은 메인주, 노스다코타주, 심지어 캐나다 등 멀리서 동일한 이곳 숲에 왔습니다.

무게는 겨우 1센트 동전의 1/5정도밖에 안되지만 엄청난 날개 짓은 마치 비가 내리는 소리처럼 들립니다.

베테랑 환경보호론자인 빌 툰 씨에게 이곳은 대단히 멋지면서 동시에 근심을 주는 장소입니다.
이곳 보호지역에서 겨울을 나는 호랑나비는 대략 2억 5천만 마리로 추정됩니다.
꽤 많은 것처럼 들리고 분명 많아 보이지만, 15년 전 약 10억 마리의 호랑나비가 있었다고 상상해 보십시오.
문제는 바로 호랑나비들이 따뜻하게 하기 위해 모여들던 이 거대한 전나무들이 잘려나가고 있다는 겁니다.
이곳은 2004년 나비들의 영역 옆에 위치한 숲입니다.
그러나 2008년까지 숲의 모습은 이랬습니다.

숲과 같은 피난처가 없다면 수백 마리의 나비들이 얼어 죽을 수도 있습니다.
한해 평균 최고 15%에 달합니다.
올해는 좋지 못한 날씨로 50% 이상 죽었습니다.
멕시코 정부는 약 140,000 에이커를 따로 호랑나비 보호구역으로 지정했습니다.
여전히 이 구역 내부에서는 연간 100,000그루 이상의 나무가 잘려나갑니다.

멕시코는 최근 해당 숲을 7% 가량 잃었는데요, 뉴저지의 2배 크기의 지역이고, 대부분 불법 벌목으로 인한 것입니다.
삼림 벌목은 호랑나비 외에 다른 것들도 위협합니다.
유역을 훼손시키며 이는 진흙사태를 일으킬 가능성이 있습니다.
이 장면은 호랑나비 보호구역에서 5마일 떨어진 곳으로 17명이 사망했습니다.
한편, 일반 가정에서조차 요리와 가정 난방을 위해, 한해 나무 40여 그루를 소비하면서 이 문제에 한몫하고 있습니다.

지금, 가는 도중에 교미를 하면서 이 숲들을 떠나고 있습니다.
여름동안 4세대가 대이니고 죽는데요. 수명이 긴 최고의 세대에 이르기 전까지 약 한 달삽니다.
나비 수명은 7개월이고 이전의 멕시코로 돌아가지 못합니다.
나비의 이동을 안전하게 지키는 것은 곧 숲을 지킨다는 의미입니다.
과연 이 호랑나비들에게 시간이 얼마나 있냐가 의문입니다.

Dictation

- ______ ______ they ______ insect royalty.
- ______ now ______ kingdom ___ ______ attack.
- ______ end tonight ______ ______ ___ nature's ______ beautiful creatures ______ greatest mysteries.
- No ______ knows why, ______ every fall, nearly every Monarch Butterfly ___ North America migrates ___ central Mexico.
- ______ now ___ Seth Doane tells ______, ______ Monarchs ______ ___ resort ___ going through ______ own metamorphosis .
- Every spring, ________ blue skies turn orange.
- ______ centuries, millions ___ M onarch butterflies ______ come ___ ________ same ancient ______ests,
- traveling ______ ___ far away ___ Maine, North Dakota, even Canada.
- They weigh ______ ___ fifth ___ ___ penny,

- ______ ______ many flapping wings ______ sound ______ falling rain.
- ______ veteran conservationist, Bill Toone, _______ site __ both awesome ______ troubling.
- _________ ______ __ estimated 250 million M onarch butterflies _______ winter __ _______ preserve.
- _______ sounds ______ __ lot , __ certainly looks ______ __ lot,
- ______ imagine 15 ______ ago , ________ ______ nearly ______ billion.
- ______ _________ __ _________ giant fir trees ________ M onarch s huddle ______ warmth ______ being ______ down.
- _______ ______ ______ ______est ______ __ ______ butterfly grounds __ 2004.
- __ 2008, __ looked ______ _______.
- Without cover, millions __ butterflies ______ freeze __ death .
- __ __ average _______, __ __ 15 % .
- _______ _______, bad weather killed _______ _______ 50 % .
- ______ Mexican government set aside ________ 140,000 acres __ __ protected zone ______ ______ M onarch B utterflies.
- Still, ______ _______ zone, every _______, _______ _______ 100,000 trees ______ ______ down.
- Mexico recently lost nearly 7 % __ ______ ______ests, __ area twice

______ size ___ New Jersey,

- much ___ ___ ______ illegal logging.
- De______estation threatens _______ _______ Monarchs.
- ___ destroys watersheds _________ ______ cause mudslides.
- _______ ______, ______ miles ______ ______ butterfly sanctuary killed 17 people.
- ______ even average families contribute ___ ______ _________,
- consuming _________ 40 trees ___ _______ ___ cook ______ heat _______ homes.
- Now, Monarchs ______ leaving _________ ______ests, mating along ______ way.
- ______ summer, four generations will ___ born ______ die,
- ______ living _________ ___ month ______ ___ super generation arrives.
- They'll live seven months, ______ having never _______ ___ Mexico ______.
- Saving ______ migration means saving ______ ______est.
- ______ question ___ , ______ much ______ ___ _________ M onarchs really _______?
- Seth Doane, CBS News, Michoacan, Mexico.

10

Debating Creationism or Evolution & 3-D Problems

Still ahead on World News, the leading bible scholar takes a surprising stand on evolution.

A new flashpoint in the culture wars.

This is ABC World News with Diane Sawyer brought to you by Frosted Mini-Wheats.

There's a surprising twist tonight in one of the flashing point debates of our time.

Is life as we know it the result of creationism or evolution?

The theory that all species have evolved from a common ancestor.

One of America's leading evangelical Christian scholars recently declared that he agreed with the scientists.

He was not prepared for what happened next.

Here's Dan Harris.

The story of creation in the book of Genesis, God creating man, Adam and Eve in the Garden of Eden, is a bedrock belief for many Christians. Two thirds of Americans say it is literally true.

So it created an uproar when the author and respected conservative evangelical Bible scholar Dr. Bruce Wakie said this about the overwhelming evidence for evolution.

“To deny that reality will make us a cult. Some odd group that's not really interacting with the real world.”

Almost immediately after that video was posted on the web, Dr. Wakie was labeled a heretic and anti-Christian.

“I believe what he is saying ultimately undermines the authority of God's word.”

Even though Dr. Wakie had the video pull down and repeatedly made clear that he thinks you can believe in both evolution and the inerrancy of the Bible, the attacks kept coming.

So last week, Wakie resigned from the seminary in Florida where he had taught for more than a decade.

But conservatives insist that undermining God's Word is leading to society's moral decay.

“If there's not an absolute authority which we can trust, then everything else is just opinion.”

Dr. Wakie has found a new job at another conservative seminary.
But the age-old tension between science and fake is only likely to increase and both sides agree the stakes couldn't be higher.
Dan harris, ABC News.

And still ahead, did this little pebble cause this spectacular light show?
The hunt tonight for a meteor light.
Startling health warning from one of the company's rolling out the next big thing in television sets that show programming in 3-D.
SAMSUNG is telling consumers that some viewers may experience an epileptic seizure or stroke when watching certain programs and video games in 3-D.

The search is on this evening for the remnants of the streaking meteor that lit up the sky from Iowa to Michigan Wednesday night.
Meteor light hunters have been scouring southwest Wisconsin Where the radar shows fireball landed.
So far only a peanut size fragment has been found.
Scientists think it was part of the meteor, they're still awaiting more tests.

Words and Idioms

- flashpoint 인화점 (비유적)화약고
  - Tension in the city is rapidly reaching **flashpoint**.
  그 도시 내의 긴장 상태가 급속히 일촉즉발의 상황으로 치닫고 있다
- evangelical 복음주의
- Genesis 창세기
- bedrock 튼튼한 기반
  - The poor suburbs traditionally formed the **bedrock** of the party's support.
  그 가난한 교외 지역이 전통적으로 그 당의 지지 기반을 형성했다.
- uproar 대소동
  - Her comments provoked (an) **uproar** from the audience.
  그녀의 논평이 청중들로부터 소란을 불러일으켰다.
- cult 광신 숭배
  - An extraordinary personality **cult** had been created around the leader.
  그 지도자를 둘러싸고 터무니없는 인물 숭배 의식이 형성되어 있었다.
- odd 이상한
  - There's something **odd** about that man.
  저 남자는 뭔가 특이한 데가 있다.
- interacting 소통하다
  - When you are **interacting** with clients, full business attire is required.
  고객들과 만나 상담을 할 때는 완전 정장 차림이어야 합니다.

- heretic 이단자
  - He was excommunicated from the church as a **heretic.**
    그는 이단자로 몰려 교회에서 추방되었다
- inerrancy 성서 무오설, 잘못이 없음
  - I am arguing for the authority of Scripture, not **inerrancy.**
    나는 성경의 무오설이 아니라 권위를 주장하고 있는 것이다.
- seminary 신학대학원
- decay 부패
  - The landlord had let the building fall into **decay.**
    집주인이 그 건물을 부식되도록 내버려 둔 상태였다.
- epileptic seizure 간질발작
  - The **leading** bible scholar **takes a surprising stand on evolution.**
    * **leading**은 '선도하는, 탁월한, 주요한 등'이고, **take one's stand on**은 '~ 한 입장을 취하다'는 의미가 있다 .
  - There's a **surprising twist** tonight in one of the flashing point debates of our time.
    * surprising twist은 상대가 전혀 예상치 못한 결과 등을 나타낼 때 사용하는 표현으로, 영화에서 **a surprising plot twist** 표현은 '반전'을 의미한다.
  - The stakes couldn't be higher.
    * **higher stakes**는 내기에서 판돈이 높아진다는 의미로 '중대한 이해 관계, 큰 부담 등'을 나타낸다.

번역 창조론과 진화론 논쟁 & 3D 문제점들

계속해서 월드 뉴스 전해드립니다. 저명한 성경학자가 진화론에 대해 놀라운 입장을 밝혔습니다.

문화 전쟁에서 (갈등의) 새로운 화약고가 될 것 같습니다.

다이앤 소여 앵커와 함께 프로스티드 미니 휘츠 협찬으로 진행되는 ABC 월드 뉴스입니다.

이 시대에 일촉즉발 위기상황을 몰고 올 논쟁 중 하나로 오늘 저녁 뜻밖의 놀라운 소식이 있습니다.

우리가 아는 바와 같이 생명은 창조론의 결과일까요, 아니면 진화론의 결과일까요?

모든 종이 공통된 조상으로부터 진화했다는 이론입니다.

미국의 주요한 복음주의 크리스천 학자 한 명이 최근 과학자들 의견에 동의한다고 선언했습니다.

그는 향후 일어날 사건에 미처 준비되지 않은 상태였습니다.

댄 해리스 기자가 전해드립니다.

에덴동산에서 아담과 하와를 창조했다는 창세기의 창조설은 수많은 크리스천들의 근본 믿음입니다.

따라서 작가 겸 존경받는 보수적인 복음주의 성경신학자인 브루스 월키 박사가 진화론의 강력한 증거에 대해 이 같은 말을 하자 엄청난 논란이 불거졌습니다.

"그 현실을 부정한다면 우리를 광신적 종교집단으로 만드는 겁니다. 진짜 세상과 진정으로 소통하지 못하는 이상한 집단인 것입니다."

관련 동영상이 웹에 게시되자마자 월키 박사는 이단자 내지 반기독교 인으로 불렸습니다.

"Wakie 박사의 언급 내용은 궁극적으로 하나님 말씀의 권위를 손상시켰다 고 봅니다."
와키(Wakie) 박사가 동영상을 내린 뒤 '진화론과 성서무오성을 둘 다 믿을 수 있다고 생각한다'고 여러 차례 분명히 밝혔지만 공격은 계속되고 있습니다.
지난 주 와키 박사는 10년 이상 강의했던 플로리다의 신학대학원를 사임했습니다.
한편, 보수주의자들은 하나님 말씀을 훼손하는 것은 사회를 도덕적으로 타락시킨다고 주장했습니다.
"인간이 신뢰할 수 있는 절대적인 권위가 존재하지 않으면 모든 것이 그저 의견에 불과합니다."

와키 박사는 다른 보수주의 신학대학원에 새 일자리를 얻었습니다.
한편, 과학과 사기 간의 오랜 긴장이 커지겠지만 양측 모두 부담감이 커집니다.
ABC 뉴스, 댄 해리스 기자였습니다.
이 작은 자갈로 눈부신 불빛 쇼를 연출했을까요?
오늘 저녁, 유성 불꽃을 추적합니다.
3D 프로그램을 내보내는 TV 부문에서 차세대 혁신제품을 대량 선보일 한 기업에서 보고한 놀라운 건강 경고 소식입니다.
삼성은 3D로 특정 프로그램을 시청하거나 비디오 게임을 할 경우 일부 시청자들이 간질 혹은 발작 증세를 보일 수 있다고 소비자들에게 경고했습니다.

수요일 저녁 아이오와 주에서 미시건 주까지 하늘을 밝힌, 번개처럼 빠른 유성의 잔여물을 계속 추적 중입니다.
유성 불빛을 쫓는 사람들은 위스콘신 주 남서부 지역을 샅샅이 조사하고 있습니다.
그 지역은 레이더가 유성이 떨어진 장면을 포착한 곳입니다.

지금까지 땅콩 크기만 한 파편만 발견됐습니다.

과학자들은 파편이 유성의 일부일 것이라고 판단하고 있고, 더 많은 테스트를 대기하고 있습니다.

Dictation

- ______ ahead ___ ________ News, _____ leading bible scholar takes ___ surprising ______ ___ evolution.
- ___ new flashpoint ___ _____ culture wars.
- ______ ___ ABC ________ News ______ Diane Sawyer brought ___ _______ ___ Frosted Mini-Wheats.
- ___________ ___ surprising twist tonight ___ ______ ___ _____ flashing point debates ___ _____ time.
- ___ ______ ___ ______ know ___ _____ result ___ creationism ______ evolution?
- _____ theory ______ all species ______ evolved ______ ___ common ancestor.
- ______ ___ America's leading evangelical Christian scholars recently declared ______ ______ agreed ______ _____ scientists.
- ______ _____ not prepared _____ ______ happened _____.

- __________ Dan Harris.
- _____ ________ ___ creation ___ _____ ________ ___ Genesis , God creating ______, Adam _____ Eve ___ _____ Garden ___ Eden,
- ___ ___ bedrock belief _____ many Christians. Two thirds ___ Americans ________ ___ ___ literally true.
- So ___ created ___ uproar _______ _____ author _____ respected conservative evangelical bible scholar Dr. Bruce Wakie
- ______ _______ about _____ overwhelming evidence _____ evolution.
- "___ deny _______ reality _______ ______ us ___ cult .
- _______ odd group __________ not really interacting _______ _____ real ________."
- Almost immediately _______ _______ video _____ posted ___ _____ web, Dr. Wakie _____ labeled ___ heretic _____ ______-Christian.
- "___ believe _______ _______ ___ saying ultimately undermines _____ authority ___ god's word."
- Even though Dr. Wakie _____ _____ video pull down _____ repeatedly made clear
- _______ _______ thinks ________ _______ believe ___ both evolution _____ _____ inerrancy ___ _____ bible,
- _____ attacks _______ coming.
- So _______ week, Wakie resigned _______ _____ seminary ___ Florida

________ ______ _____ taught _____ ______ ______ ___ decade.

- _____ conservatives insist ______ undermining God's Word ___ leading ___ society's moral decay .
- "____ ___________ not ___ absolute authority ______ ______ ______ trust, ______ everything else ___ ______ opinion."
- Dr. Wakie ______ found ___ new job ___ ______ conservative seminary.
- _____ _____ ______-old tension between science _____ ______ ___ only likely ___ increase
- ____ both sides agree _____ stakes couldn't ___ higher.
- Dan harris, ABC News.
- ____ ______ ahead, ______ ______ little pebble cause ______ spectacular ______ ______?
- ____ ______ tonight _____ ___ ______ ______.
- Startling health warning ______ ______ ___ _____ company's rolling ______ _____ _____ big _______ ___ television sets ______ ______ programming ___ 3-D.
- SAMSUNG ___ telling consumers ______ ______ viewers ______ experience ___ epileptic seizure ______ stroke
- ______ watching certain programs _____ video games ___ 3-D.
- _____ search ___ ___ ______ evening _____ _____ remnants ___ _____ streaking ______ ______ ______ ___ _____ ______ ______ Iowa ___

Michigan Wednesday night.

- ______ ______ hunters ______ ______ scouring southwest Wisconsin
- ________ ____ radar ______ fireball landed.
- So far only ___ peanut size fragment ______ ______ found.
- Scientists ______ __ ____ ______ __ ____ ______, ____________ ______ awaiting ______ tests.

11

Daniel Tammet's genius memory in action

Amazing life. After you see this man's memory in action, all you'll say is "wow."
From ABC News headquarters, this is ABC World News with Diane Sawyer.
And now we want to show you the latest accomplishment from a man whose mind has amazed us time and again.
He has Asperger Syndrome. His brain is simply acrobatic.
Our Nick Watt watched him learn an impossible new language at impossible speed.

31-year-old Daniel Tammet is on the outside and unremarkable young man.
But like Clark Kent, behind Tammet's bookish exterior that lies a superhuman gift .
One of the most extraordinary brains our planet has ever seen.
Scientists have tested Tammet's memory.
They had him take a look at pi.

“You read through them at once?” “Yeah.” “One time only?”

He memorized the first 22,000 digits of pi, and then begins reciting the numbers back in order.

In a normal brain, different parts don't talk to each other.

In Tammet's brain, they do.

That's why he sees numbers as beautiful shapes and color.

Not only our numbers a gift, and so our words.

He knows eight languages, and we watched him pick up one more.

Off to Reykjavik, Iceland where Tammet touches down with a final challenge to learn Icelandic.

Remember the name of that Icelandic volcano that was in the news?

He'll have just one week.

Tammet appeared on Icelandic TV. A live talk show.

Holy cow! He nailed it.

Unbelievable! How do you say wow in Icelandic?

And you can see more of Daniel Tammet's amazing abilities along with other people capable of things you do not believe as possible.

Tonight on a special 20/20.

And don't forget Good Morning America. George Stephanopoulos live from the Gulf tomorrow morning.

We'll see you back here tomorrow night.

Words and Idioms

- time and (time) again 되풀이해서
  - They say animal experiments have shown **time and time again** that clones turn out to be deformed or defective.
    과학자들은 복제 동물이 기형을 일으키거나 결함이 있다는 것이 수차례의 동물 실험을 통해 판명됐다고 말합니다.
- acrobatic 곡예의
  - The audience gave the acrobat a big round of applause for his **acrobatic** performance.
    관객들은 곡예사의 묘기에 박수를 보냈다
- unremarkable 평범한
- an unremarkable life 특별할 것 없는 삶
- bookish 책을 좋아하는
  - **Bookish** people very often like to stay at home.
    책을 좋아하는 사람들은 흔히 집에 있기를 좋아한다.
- extraordinary 놀라운
- reciting 암송하는
- Holy cow! 저런 어쩜

- **Holy cow**, look at the size of that set.
  대단하군요, 정말 크네요.

• He nailed it 성공하다

- He knows eight languages, and we watched him **pick up** one more.
  * watch는 지각동사로 [지각동사 + 목 + 동사원형 (-ing)]의 형태가 되며, 여기에서 **pick up**은 '(지식, 외국어)를 익히다'는 의미로 쓰였다.
- Tammet **appeared** on Icelandic TV.
  * **appear**는 목적어가 필요 없는 자동사로 1)~에 출현하다, 등장하다 2)~처럼 보이다(=seem) 등의 의미가 있다.

번역 다니엘 타멧 천재 청년의 기억력

놀라운 삶입니다. 이 남성의 기억이 작용하는 모습을 보시면 모두 '와!' 하고 탄성을 지를 것입니다.
ABC 뉴스 국제부에서 다이앤 소여 앵커가 ABC 월드 뉴스를 전해드립니다.
계속해서 우리를 깜짝 놀라게 한 머리를 가진 한 남성이 이룬 최근 업적을 보여드리겠습니다.
그는 아스퍼거 증후군을 겪고 있습니다. 그의 두뇌는 가히 곡예 수준입니다.
닉 와트 기자는 그가 불가능한 속도로 불가능한 새로운 언어를 학습하는 모습을 지켜봤습니다.

31세인 다니엘 타멧씨는 외관상 평범한 청년입니다.
한편, 클락 켄트 (주_영화 '수퍼맨'의 평범한 모습)처럼, 책을 좋아하는 타멧씨의 외관상 모습 뒤에는 수퍼맨과 같은 재능이 있습니다.

지구상에서 목격된 가장 뛰어난 두뇌를 가진 인물 중 한 사람입니다.
과학자들은 타밋씨의 암기력을 테스트했습니다.
그들은 타밋씨에게 π (파이)를 슬쩍 한번 보라고 했습니다.
"한번에 읽었나요?", "네.", "한번 뿐이라고요?"
그는 파이의 첫 22,000개 숫자를 기억한 다음 뒤에서부터 순서대로 숫자를 암송했습니다.

일반적인 두뇌에서 여러 다른 부분은 서로 소통하지 못합니다.
그러나 타밋씨의 뇌에서는 그런 일이 일어납니다.
이런 이유로 그에게는 숫자들이 아름다운 형태와 색깔로 보여집니다.
숫자는 재능일 뿐만 아니라 단어도 마찬가지입니다.
그는 8 가지 언어를 압니다. 그리고 우리는 그가 언어 하나를 더 학습하는 모습을 지켜봤습니다.
타밋씨가 아이슬란드어를 배우기 위해 마지막 도전장을 내면서 도착한 아이슬란드의 레이캬비크로 향했습니다.
뉴스에 나왔던 아이슬란드 화산 이름을 기억하십니까?
그에게 주어진 시간은 단 1주일입니다.
타밋 씨는 아이슬란드 TV에 출연했습니다. 생방송 토크쇼였습니다.

저런 대단하군요! 해냈습니다!
믿겨지지 않습니다. 아이슬란드어로 '와'를 어떻게 말할까요?
오늘 저녁 특집 프로그램 20/20 에서 도무지 믿을 수 없는 능력을 가진 다른 사람들과 함께 다니얼 태밋 씨의 놀라운 능력을 보다 상세히 볼 수 있습니다.
〈굿모닝 아메리카〉도 놓치지 마시기 바랍니다. 내일 아침, 멕시코 만에서 조지 스테파노풀로스 기자가 생방송으로 보도합니다.
내일 저녁 다시 뵙겠습니다.

Dictation

- Amazing _____. _______ _____ _____ _____ man's memory ___ action, _____ _____'ll say ___ "wow."
- _____ ABC News headquarters, _____ ___ ABC ______ News _____ Diane Sawyer.
- _____ now ___ _____ ___ show _____ _____ ______ accomplishment _____ ___ man whose mind _____ amazed ___ ______ _____ ______ .
- ___ _____ Asperger Syndrome . _____ brain ___ simply acrobatic .
- _____ Nick Watt _________ him learn ___ impossible _____ language ___ impossible speed.
- 31-_______-_____ Daniel Tammet ___ ___ _____ outside _____ unremarkable young man.
- _____ _____ Clark Kent, _____ Tammet's bookish exterior _____ lies ___ superhuman gift .
- _____ ___ _____ most extraordinary brains _____ planet _____ ever ________.
- Scientists _____ tested Tammet's memory.
- _____ _____ him _____ ___ look ___ pi.
- "_____ read _________ _____ ___ once?" "Yeah." "_____ _______ _____?"

- ___ memorized _____ _____ 22,000 digits ___ pi,
- _____ _____ begins reciting _____ numbers _______ ___ order.
- ___ ___ normal brain, different parts ______ talk ___ each _______.
- ___ Tammet's brain, ______ do.
- ________ _____ ___ sees numbers ___ beautiful shapes _____ color.
- ______ ______ _____ numbers ___ gift, _____ ___ _____ words.
- ___ knows eight languages, _____ ___ __________ him pick ___ _____ _______.
- Off ___ Reykjavik, Iceland ________ Tammet touches ______ _____ ___ final challenge ___ learn Icelandic.
- Remember _____ name ___ _____ Icelandic volcano _____ _____ ___ _____ news?
- ________ ______ ______ _____ week.
- Tammet appeared ___ Icelandic TV. ___ live talk show.
- Holy cow! ___ nailed ___.
- Unbelievable! ______ do ______ say wow ___ Icelandic?
- _____ ______ ______ ______ _______ ___ Daniel Tammet's amazing abilities
- along _____ ________ people capable ___ _________ ______ do ______ believe ___ possible.

- __________ __ __ special 20/20.
- ____ _____ forget Good Morning America. George Stephanopoulos live ____ ____ Gulf tomorrow morning.
- _______ _____ _____ ______ ______ tomorrow night.

12

US High Schools dropout rate

This is a time of year when a lot of proud parents watch their children receive their high school diplomas.

But it's shocking to learn how many kids in this country never get one.

A loss not only for them, but for society and the economy as well.

Now thanks to new programs on both sides of the country, there's real hope for the future.

Bill Whittaker continues our series: Where America Stands.

A typical day in the schools of Philadelphia.

And Sarae White is an all too typical student.

She stopped going to school last year, "The teachers didn't care, the students didn't care," and was on her way to becoming one more dropout.

"It seemed like nobody cared. So why should I?"

In Philadelphia, the country's sixth largest city, about one of every three students fails to graduate about the national average.

The country's report card on dropouts, a dismal D.

Of the 4 million students who enter high school every year, almost 1.3 million will drop out before graduation.

That's 7,000 every school day, one dropout every 26 seconds.

Michael Piscal, founded View Park Prep. Charter School in Los Angeles,

"It's not working for teachers, it's not working for the students, it's not working for society.”

The dropout problem is even worse in big cities.

Almost half of all students in the country's 50 largest school districts fail to get high school diplomas.

30 years ago, the US led the world in high school graduation.

Today, we rank 18th among industrial nations.

The reasons why? As varied as the dropouts themselves.

Family problems, pregnancy, boredom, safety.

Why should what happens here matter to every American?

Well, besides the intrinsic value of education itself, when one American lacks an education, it hurts us all in the wallet.

Dropouts cost taxpayers more than $8 billion annually in public assistance programs like food stamps.

High school dropouts earn about $10,000 less a year than workers with diplomas.

That's $300 billion in lost lifetime earnings for each class of dropouts.

They're more likely to be unemployed.

15 % are out of work versus a national average of 10%.

They also are more likely to be incarcerated.

Almost 60% of federal inmates are high school dropouts.

"You have high schools in Los Angeles that send more kids to prison than they graduate kids from college.

It's time for a radical, radical change."

Michael Piscal has found a solution.

The former English teacher at the most rigorous private school in Los Angeles opened View Park Prep. 15 years ago, bringing the private school's curriculum to one of south LA's toughest neighborhoods.

"What's best for the rich kids is best for all kids."

At the local public schools, more than 50% of students drop out.

Words and Idioms

- dropout 중퇴자

 - In the past 20-30 years attendance rates have decreased and **dropout** rates have decreased.
 지난 20~30년에 걸쳐서 출석율과 중퇴자 비율이 줄어들었다.

- boredom 따분함

 - Television helps to relieve the **boredom** of the long winter evenings.
 텔레비전은 긴 겨울밤의 심심함을 달래는 데 도움이 된다.

- intrinsic 본질적인 /
 the intrinsic value of education 교육의 고유한[본질적인] 가치

 - These tasks were repetitive, lengthy and lacking any **intrinsic** interest.
 이들 과업은 반복적이고 지루하며 고유한 흥미가 결여되어 있었다.

- incarcerated 감금하다

 - They **incarcerated** the man, but many people believed that he was innocent.
 그들이 그 남자를 투옥했지만, 많은 사람들은 그가 무죄라고 믿었다.

- rigorous 엄격한

 - The work failed to meet their **rigorous** standards.
 그 작업은 그들의 엄격한 기준을 충족시키지 못했다.

 - She stopped **going** to school last year, "The teachers didn't care, the students didn't care," and was **on her way to** becoming one more dropout.
 * [stop 동사 + ing]는 문법적으로 동명사를 목적으로 '- 하던 것을 멈추다'로 to부정사를 목적어로 갖는 '~하기 위해 멈추다'는 뜻을

가진 [stop to+ 동사원형]구문과 구별한다. on one's way to 는 '~로 가는 길(도중)에'이다.

- They also are more likely to **be incarcerated.**
  * likely 는 '~ 할 것 같은'의 의미로 [be likely to+ 동사원형]은 '~할 것 같다'는 의미이다. 타동사 Incarcerate는 투옥하다 이지만 '투옥되다'라는 의미를 만들기 위해서는 수동태(be + 과거분사)로 써야 한다.

번역 미국 고등학생 중퇴율

자랑스러운 수많은 부모님들이 이들 자녀가 고교 졸업장을 수여하는 모습을 보게 되는 때입니다.
한편, 미국 내 많은 학생들이 졸업장을 받지 못한다는 사실은 충격적입니다.
이들 뿐만 아니라 사회 및 경제 부문에도 손실입니다.
양측의 새로운 프로그램 덕분에 미래에 대한 희망이 있습니다.
빌 휘태커 기자가 본사 시리즈 - 미국은 지금 (Where America Stands) 을 계속 보도합니다.

필라델피아의 학교에서 볼 수 있는 전형적인 하루입니다.
사라 화이트는 매우 전형적인 학생입니다.
이 학생은 작년에 학교를 그만뒀습니다. "선생님들은 관심이 없으셨고, 학생들도 신경 쓰지 않았어요."
그리고 또 한 명의 중퇴자가 되었습니다.
아무도 신경 쓰지 않는 것 같았습니다. 그렇다면 제가 왜 굳이 학교를 다녀야 하나요?

필라델피아는 전국에서 6번째 가장 큰 도시로 약 1/3은 졸업을 하지 못하며 대략 미국 평균치입니다. 고교 중퇴에 대한 미국의 성적표는 참담하게도 D 입니다 .

매년 고등학교에 입학하는 학생 4백만 명 중 130만명 정도는 졸업이전에 중퇴합니다.
매일 7천명에 해당하는 수치이며 26초당 한 명이 중퇴합니다.
마이클 피스칼 씨는 로스앤젤레스에 위치한 뷰파크 프렙 차터스쿨(Charter School)을 설립했습니다.
"교사에게도 제 역할을 못하고 있습니다. 학생, 그리고 사회에도 제 역할을 못하고 있는 겁니다." 중퇴 문제는 대도시가 훨씬 심각합니다.
미국 50개 학군의 학생 절반가량은 고교 졸업장을 못 받습니다.
30년 전 미국은 고교 졸업 부문에서 전 세계에서 선두에 섰습니다.
그러나 오늘날 산업 국가 가운데 18위를 차지하고 있습니다.

이유가 무엇일까요? 중퇴 이유는 제각각 다양합니다.
가족 문제, 임신, 지루한 학교 생활, 안전 등의 이유입니다.
이곳에서 발생하는 문제가 모든 미국인에게 왜 중요할까요?
교육 그 자체 본질적인 문제와 함께 미국인의 교육 부재는 우리 모두에게 지갑에 큰 타격을 줍니다. 중퇴는 푸드스탬프와 같은 공공보조 프로그램으로 납세자들에게 연간 80억 달러 이상의 비용을 부담시킵니다.
고등학교 중퇴자들은 졸업장을 소지한 근로자보다 연간 수입이 10,000달러가량 적습니다. 실업 상태에 처할 확률도 더 높습니다 .
실업률이 미 평균 10%인데 반해 이들은 15%입니다.

또한, 수감될 확률도 높습니다.
연방정부 재소자 중 60%가 고교 중퇴자들입니다.

"로스앤젤레스에는 대학에서 졸업을 하는 경우보다 감옥에 수감되는 학생이 더 많은 고등학교들이 있습니다."

급진적인, 급진적인 변화가 필요한 시점입니다.

마이클 파스칼 씨는 해결책을 찾았습니다.

로스앤젤레스에서 가장 엄격한 사립학교의 전직 영어 교사가 15년 전 뷰파크 프렙 학교를 열었고, 사립학교의 커리큘럼을 남부 LA에서 가장 난감한 동네 중 한 곳에 가져왔습니다.

"부유한 학생들에게 최상의 것은 모든 학생들에게도 가장 좋은 것이죠."

해당 지역 공립학교에는 50% 이상의 학생이 중퇴했습니다.

Dictation

- _____ ___ ___ _______ ___ _______ _______ ___ ______ ___ proud parents watch ________ children receive ________ ______ __________ diplomas.
- _____ ______ shocking ___ learn ______ many kids ___ _____ country ______ ______ _____.
- ___ loss ______ ______ _____ ______, _____ _____ society _____ _____ economy ___ ______.
- Now ________ ___ _____ programs ___ ______ sides ___ _____ country,
- ________'s ______ ___________ _____ _____ future.
- Bill Whittaker continues _____ series: ________ America Stands.

- ___ typical day ___ _____ schools ___ Philadelphia.
- _____ Sarae White ___ ___ ______ too typical student .
- She ___________ ______ ___ ___________ _____ _______ , "_____ teachers didn't care, _____ students didn't care,"
- _____ _____ ___ _____ way ___ becoming _____ _______ dropout .
- " ___ seemed _____ n obody cared . ___ _____ ______ ___?"
- ___ Philadelphia, _____ country's sixth largest city ,
- _________ _____ ___ _________ three students fails ___ graduate _________ _____ national average.
- _____ country's _____ card ___ dropouts, ___ dismal D .
- ___ _____ 4 million students _____ enter ______ ___________ _________ ______, almost 1.3 million will drop ______ before graduation.
- ________ 7,000 _________ ___________ day , _____ dropout _________ 26 seconds.
- Michael Piscal, founded View Park Prep . Charter ___________ ___ Los Angeles ,
- "______ ______ working _____ teachers, ______ ______ working _____ _____ students , ______ ______ working _____ society. ”
- _____ dropout __________ ___ ______ worse ___ big cities.
- Almost ______ ___ ______ students ___ _____ country's 50 largest ___________ districts

- fail ___ ______ ______ ___________ diploma s .
- 30 _______ ______ , _____ ___ led _____ _______ ___ ______ ___________ graduation.
- Today , ___ rank 18th among industrial nations.
- _____ reasons _____? ___ varied ___ _____ dropouts themselves.
- _______ problems, pregnancy, boredom , safety.
- _____ ______ _____ happens _______ matter ___ _________ American?
- _____, b esides _____ intrinsic value ___ education itself,
- _______ _____ American lack s ___ education , ___ hurts ___ ______ ___ _____ wallet.
- Dropouts cost taxpayers _______ _____ $8 billion annually ___ public assistance programs ______ food stamps.
- ______ ___________ dropouts earn _________ $10 ,000 less ___ _______ _____ workers _____ diplomas.
- ________ $300 billion ___ ______ lifetime earnings _____ each ______ ___ dropouts .
- __________ _______ likely ___ ____ unemployed .
- 15 % ______ _______ ___ ______ versus ___ national average ___ 10 % .
- ______ ____ ______ _______ likely ___ ____ incarcerated .
- Almost 60 % ___ federal inmates ______ ______ __________ dropouts.

- "_____ _____ _____ schools ___ Los Angeles ____ send ______ kids ___ prison ____ _____ graduate kids ____ __________ .
- _____ ______ ____ __ radical, radical _________."
- Michael Piscal ____ __________ __ solution.
- ____ former English teacher __ ____ most rigorous private __________ ___ Los Angeles
- opened View Park Prep . 15 ______ _____,
- bringing ____ private __________'s curriculum __ ____ __ south LA's toughest neighborhoods.
- "_______ best ____ ____ rich kids __ best ____ _____ kids."
- __ ____ local public schools, ______ ____ 50 % __ students drop ______.

13

Iceland's Ice and Volcano

We're back tonight with a closer look at a nation we've all been watching closely lately because it's quite literally a hotbed of volcanic activity.
Tonight while flights around the world are still getting back to normal, in Iceland, they worried that a wind shift might shut down their major airports.
It's an active environment there because Iceland sits on top of what may be the largest crack in the crust to the earth anywhere on earth.
Our chief science correspondent Robert Bazel is there and got this close-up look.

This current eruption is one more demonstration of the earth's awesome fire power in this land of volcanos.
Iceland, the size of Kentucky, has 35 active volcanoes with an eruption on average every two or three years.

It is a place where much of the surface is very close to the immense heat from the center of the planet.
These steam baths were throughout the country occurred because water sips into the earth and heats the molten rock which is right beneath the surface.

Iceland's earth structure comes from the same forces that produce earthquakes, tsunamis and volcanoes.
The huge sections of the earth called plates that are in constant motion.
This island nation straddles a plate boundary called the Mid Atlantic ridge.
This is actually a fault line.
On this side is the North American plate. On that side is the European plate.
They're moving apart at the rate of about one inch a year.
That ever expanding fissure allows the molten rock from within the earth to rise constantly.

For seismologist like Bryndis Brandsdottir, the challenge is enormous.
"There's lots of activity, you know, you don't have to wait to run for the data.
You usually, you know, you have too much work, too much data to."
The volcanoes have produced some spectacular distance.
And geothermal heat offers great opportunities for recreation as well as warmth and electricity for 80% of the nation's houses.
But it also poses a danger that we now know can affect much of the world.
Robert Bazel, NBC News, Iceland.

Words and Idioms

- hotbed 온상

  – We should not allow the existence of destitute country that could turn into a **hotbed** of international terrorism.
  국제적인 테러의 온상으로 변할 수 있기 때문에 우리는 빈곤한 국가의 존재를 좌시해서는 안 된다.

- crust 지각

  – The thinner the dough the thinner the **crust**.
  반죽이 얇을수록 빵껍질도 얇아진다.

- awesome 무시무시한 / 굉장한/ 아주 멋진

  – My step-dad though, he is definitely an **awesome** guy.
  새 아빠 이지만, 그는 대단히 멋진 남자이다.

- immense 거대한

  – She has risen from humble origins to **immense** wealth.
  그녀는 하찮은 집안 출신에서 거부가 되었다.

- sips 조금씩 마시다, 조금씩 스며들다/ 한 모금

  – He took a **sip** of the medicine and screwed up his face.
  그가 그 약을 한 모금 마시더니 얼굴을 찡그렸다.

- molten 녹은

- straddles 두발을 벌리다.

  – The mountains **straddle** the French-Swiss border.
  그 산맥은 프랑스-스위스 국경을 가로지르고 있다.

- fault line 단층선

- fissure 갈라진 틈

- The **fissure** was discovered about five years ago, leaving many scientists baffled at its very existence.
  갈라진 틈은 약 5년 전에 발견되었고, 많은 과학자들이 그것의 존재에 대해 매우 당황스러워하게 했다.

• seismologist 지진학자

- It is a place **where** much of the surface is very close to the immense heat from the center of the planet.
  * where는 관계부사로 [접속사 + 부사구]의 역할을 하며, 선행사인 장소(a place)에 대한 정보를 제공한다.
- That ever expanding fissure **allows** the molten rock from within the earth **to rise** constantly.
  * allow는 목적격 보어로 to 부정사를 사용한다. 이때 '목적어가 ~하도록 허용하다'로 해석한다. 이와 같이 **목적격 보어를 to 부정사로 취하는 동사**로는 ask, get, advise, tell, order, persuade 등이 있다.

번역 아이슬란드의 얼음과 화산

오늘 저녁에는 최근 면밀히 주시해 온 한 국가 소식을 다시 자세히 살펴보겠습니다. 이는 말 그대로 화산 활동의 온상지이기 때문입니다.
전 세계 비행기들이 정상화되고 있지만 아이슬란드에서는 바람의 이동이 주요 공항을 폐쇄시킬지도 모른다며 걱정했습니다.
그곳은 화산 활동이 활성화된 환경입니다. 지구상 어느 곳이든 가장 큰 지각균열이 일어날 가능성이 있는 최정상부에 자리 잡고 있기 때문입니다.
본사의 로버트 바젤 수석 과학기자가 현장에 나가 자세히 살펴봤습니다.

현재 폭발 모습은 이 화산지대에서 지구상의 무시무시한 화력을 잘 보여주고 있습니다.
켄터키 크기만한 아이스란드는 평균 2, 3년마다 분출하는 활화산이 35개 있습니다.
표면의 상당 부분은 지구 중앙에서 나오는 거대한 열과 매우 가까운 곳입니다.
이러한 증기탕은 전국 도처에 있습니다. 물이 땅 속으로 조금씩 스며들고 , 표면 바로 아래의 녹은 암석을 가열시킵니다.

아이슬란드의 지표 구조는 지진, 쓰나미 및 화산을 만드는 동일한 힘에서 나옵니다.
지구의 거대한 구획들은 판이라고 부르는데 지속적으로 이동 중입니다.
이것은 실제 단층선입니다. 이쪽에는 북미 판이 있고, 저쪽은 유럽판입니다.
판들은 한 해 약 1인치 속도로 멀어지고 있습니다.
그 확장되고 있는 갈라진 틈을 통해 지구 내에서 용암이 지속적으로 분출되고 있습니다.

브린디스 브랜스도티르와 같은 지진연구학자에게 이러한 도전은 정말 대단합니다.
"수많은 화산활동이 있습니다. 데이터를 위해 기다릴 필요가 없습니다. 당신은 평소, 할 일이 너무 많이 있습니다. 데이터가 너무 많습니다."
화산은 장관을 이루는 모습을 만듭니다.
또한, 지열은 미국 가정의 80%에 필요한 온기와 전기뿐 아니라 휴양을 즐길 수 있는 멋진 기회를 제공합니다. 하지만 이는 또한 전 세계 많은 부분에 영향을 줄 수 있는 위험성을 내포합니다.
아이슬란드에서 NBC 뉴스, 로버트 바젤 기자였습니다.

Dictation

- ________ ______ __________ _____ ___ closer look ___ ___ nation ________ _____ _____ watching closely lately
- _________ _____ quite literally ___ hotbed ___ volcanic activity.
- __________ ______ flights around _____ ______ _____ _____ getting ______ ___ normal,
- ___ Iceland, _____ worried _____ ___ wind shift might shut _____ ________ ________ airports.
- _____ ___ active environment _______ _________ Iceland sits ___ _____ ___ _____ _____ ____
- ____ largest crack ___ _____ crust ___ _____ earth anywhere ___ earth.
- ____ ______ science correspondent Robert Bazel ___ _______ _____ _____ _____ close-___ look.
- ____ current eruption ___ _____ ______ demonstration ___ _____ earth's awesome fire power ___ _____ land ___ volcanos.
- Iceland, ____ size ___ Kentucky, ____ 35 active volcanoes
- ____ ___ eruption ___ average ________ two ___ three ______.
- ___ ___ ___ place _______ _______ ___ _____ surface ___ very close ___ ____ immense heat _____ _____ center ___ _____ planet.
- _______ steam baths _____ throughout ____ country

- occurred _________ water sips _____ _____ earth
- _____ heats _____ molten rock _______ ___ right beneath _____ surface.
- Iceland's earth structure _____ _____ _____ same forces _____ produce earthquakes, tsunamis _____ volcanoes.
- _____ huge sections ___ _____ earth _____ plates _____ _____ ___ constant motion.
- _____ island nation straddles ___ plate boundary _____ _____ Mid Atlantic ridge.
- _____ ___ actually ___ fault line .
- ___ _____ side ___ _____ North American plate. ___ _____ side ___ _____ European plate.
- _________ moving apart ___ _____ _____ ___ ________ _____ inch ___ _______.
- _____ ever expanding fissure allows _____ molten rock _____ within _____ earth ___ rise constantly.
- _____ seismologist _____ Bryndis Brandsdottir , _____ challenge ___ enormous.
- "_______'s lots ___ activity, _____ _____, _____ _____ _____ ___ wait ___ run _____ _____ data.
- _____ usually, _____ _____, _____ _____ too ______ _____ , too ______ data ___. "

- _____ volcanoes ______ produced some spectacular distance.
- _____ geothermal heat offers great opportunities _____ recreation
- ___ ______ ___ warmth _____ electricity _____ 80% ___ _____ nation's houses.
- _____ ___ ____ poses ___ danger _____ ___ now ______ ______ affect _______ ___ _____ _______.
- Robert Bazel, NBC News, Iceland.

14

Misdiagnosised with a vegetative state for 23 years

Back to life. A man thought to be in a vegetative state for 23 years reveals he was aware of everything going on around him.

And the battle by the bay.

What to do about an invasion of hundreds of hundreds of hungry sea lions?

Imagine being trapped inside your own body unable to talk, but aware of everything going on around you.

For 23 years, a man in Belgium lived that nightmare.

All that time, doctors believe he was in a coma.

But as Elizabeth Palmer reports, he wasn't.

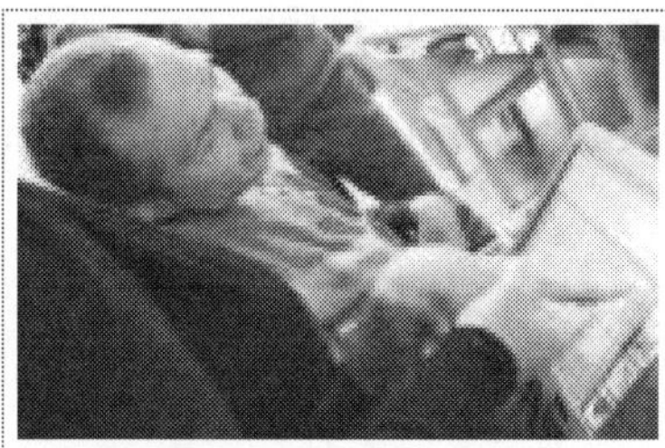

In 1983, a car accident left Ron Houben in what doctors diagnosed as a vegetative state.
Alive, but unable to feel or thinking.
And her Dr. Steven Laureys, more than 2 decades later to prove them wrong using the latest brain imaging technology.
“We put him in the PET scanner and the fMRI.
And we saw his brain was functioning normally.
So he was not vegetative. Definitely not.”

Ron's mother Fena is proud to show photos of her son before the accident.
And she never believed once injured, that he stopped feeling or hearing.
I couldn't tell, she says, when he was in a bad mood or when he was in pain.
Once doctors realized his brain was working, the challenge was how to help him communicate.
Although it's impossible to see Ron's hand move, his specially trained assistant can feel it and she translates these micro movements into words on a keyboard.

I shall never forget the day when they discovered what was really wrong with me, Ron wrote.
It was my second birth.
For Dr. Laureys, Ron's story was both thrilling and alarming.
In a study of patients diagnosed vegetative by doctors which means their life support could legally be switched off, Dr. Laurey found 40% of them showed signs of consciousness.
“I think, of course, 40% this unacceptable!
We need to do better and it's only with accurate data with objective

measurements that will be able to make the best decision for the patients."
A decision that in this case brought Ron Houben in his own words back to life.
Elizabeth Palmer, CBS News, London .

Now to a scientific milestone, 150 years ago today, Charles Darwin's on the origin of species was published.
Marking the anniversary of first edition copy sold for more than $170,000 at Christie's auction house in London.
This particular book spent decades on the shelf in an Oxford professor's bathroom until his son in law discovered its origin.

Words and Idioms

- vegetative state 식물인간상태
  - She remained in a **vegetative state.**
    그녀는 식물인간 상태에 있었다.
- coma 혼수상태
  - She drifted in and out of a deep **coma.**
    그녀는 깊은 혼수상태에 빠졌다 깨어나기를 반복했다.
- consciousness 의식
  - Slipping in and out of **consciousness**, she muttered a few words.
    그 여자는 의식이 간간이 돌아올 때면 몇 마디 말을 중얼기렸다.

- objective 객관적인
  - Owning homes is the most important **objective** of Koreans.
    내 집 장만이 한국인들의 최대 목표이다.
  - **Once** doctors realized his brain was working, the challenge was **how to** help him communicate.
    * 접속사 once 는 '일단 ~ 하면'으로 주어 + 동사가 위치한다. [의문사 + to + 동사원형]은 '~해야 할지'로 해석하고 여기에서 how to help는 '어떻게 도와야 하지, ~을 돕는 방법'으로 풀이한다.
  - For Dr. Laureys, Ron's story was both **thrilling** and **alarming**.
    * both는 상관접속사로 and와 함께 쓰인다. both A and B에서 특히, A와 B는 동일한 문법 요소가 위치해야 하므로 이 문장에서는 모두 현재분사(-ing)를 사용했다.

번역 23년간 식물인간으로 오진

삶을 되찾았습니다.

23년간 식물인간 상태라고 여겨진 한 남자가 자신 주변에 일어나는 모든 일을 인식하고 있었다는 사실이 밝혀졌습니다.

만(灣) 주변에서 벌어진 싸움입니다.

수만 마리의 굶주린 바다사자의 침략에서 무슨 일을 해야 할까요?

자신의 몸속에 갇힌 채 말할 수는 없었지만, 주변에 일어나는 모든 일들을 인식하고 있었습니다.

벨기에의 한 남성은 23년간 이 악몽 속에 살았습니다.

언제나 의료진은 그가 혼수상태에 빠져 있다고 생각했습니다.

엘리자베스 파머 기자의 보도에 따르면 그는 그렇지 않았습니다.

1983년, 차 사고를 당한 뒤 론(Ron) 후븐(Houben)은 의료진의 진단에 따라 식물인간 상태에 놓여 있었습니다.
즉, 살아있지만 느끼거나 생각할 수 없는 처지였습니다.
그리고 스티븐 로레이스(Steven Laureys)박사는 20여 년 뒤, 최신 뇌 영상 기술을 사용하여 그들의 진단이 잘못됐음을 증명했습니다.
"우리는 그에게 PET 스캐너 및 MRI 촬영을 실시했습니다."
그의 두뇌가 정상적으로 기능하고 있다는 사실을 알았습니다.
따라서 그는 식물인간이 아니었습니다. 분명 아니었습니다."

론(Ron)의 어머니 페나(Fena)씨는 자랑스럽게, 사고가 발생하기 전에 찍은 아들의 사진을 여러 장 보여줬습니다.
어머니는 아들이 다쳤을 때 아들이 감정을 느끼지 못하고 듣지 못한다고 생각해 본적이 없었습니다.
의료진이 론(Ron)의 두뇌가 제대로 기능한다는 사실을 알았을 때, 그가 의사소통 하는 방법을 도와주는 것이 도전과제였습니다.
론(Ron)의 손 움직임을 볼 수는 없지만, 특별히 훈련받은 보조사는 손 움직임을 느낄 수 있습니다.
그리고 그녀는 이러한 미세한 움직임을 키보드를 통해 단어로 해석해 줍니다.

론(Ron)은 '그들이 제게 일어나는 잘못된 사실을 발견했던 그 날을 잊지 못할 겁니다'라고 썼습니다. '제가 다시 태어난 날이었습니다.'
로레이스 박사에게 론 이야기는 전율을 느끼게 하는 동시에 경각심을 일깨웠습니다.
의료진에게 식물인간으로 진단받은 환자들에 대한 한 연구에 따르면, 이는 환자들의 생명 보조기 스위치를 합법적으로 끌 수 있음을 나타냅니다.
로레이스 박사는 이들 중 40%가 의식이 있다는 신호를 보였다는 사실을 발견했습니다.

물론 이 40%도 받아들일 수 없습니다. 의료진은 보다 잘 진단해야 합니다. 그리고 환자를 위해 최상의 결정을 내릴 수 있도록 객관적인 측정치를 갖춘 정확한 데이터가 있어야 합니다.

이 사례에서 내린 결정으로 론 후븐은 자신의 말로 표현하는 삶으로 돌아왔습니다.

런던에서 CBS 뉴스, 엘리자베스 파머 기자였습니다.

지금부터 과학 부문의 획기적인 소식을 전해드리겠습니다.

150년 전 바로 오늘, 찰스 다윈의 '종의 기원'이 출간됐습니다.

초판 사본을 기념하여 런던의 '크리스티 옥션 하우스(Christie's auction house)'에서 $170,000가 넘는 금액에 책이 팔렸습니다.

이 특별한 책은 한 옥스포드대 교수의 사위가 그 책의 출처(기원)를 발견할 때까지

욕실 선반에 수십 년간 비치되어 있었습니다.

Dictation

- ______ __ ______. __ man ________ __ __ __ __ vegetative ______ ____ 23 _____

- reveals ____ _____ _____ __ everything ______ ____ around _______.

- ____ ____ _______ __ ____ bay.

- ____ __ do ______ __ invasion __ hundreds __ hundreds __ hungry sea lions?

- ________ ______ trapped ______ _____ _____ body
- unable ___ talk, _____ _____ ___ everything ______ _____ around _____.
- _____ 23 _____, ___ man ___ Belgium lived ______ nightmare.
- ______ ______ ______, ________ _______ _____ _____ ___ ___ coma.
- _____ ___ Elizabeth Palmer ________, _____ _____.
- ___ 1983, ___ car accident ______ Ron Houben ___ _____ ________ diagnosed ___ ___ vegetative ______.
- Alive, _____ unable ___ ______ ___ thinking.
- _____ _______ Dr. St________ Laureys, _______ _____ 2 __________ later ___ prove _____ wrong using _____ _____ ________ imaging technology.
- "_____ put _______ ___ _____ PET scanner _____ _____ fMRI.
- _____ _____ saw _____ ________ _____ functioning normally.
- _____ _____ _____ not vegetative. Definitely not."
- Ron's ________ Fena ___ proud ___ ________ photos ___ _______ _____ _______ _____ accident.
- _____ ______ _____ ________ once injured, ______ _____ stopped feeling ___ hearing.
- __ ______ ______, ______ ______, _____ _____ _____ ___ ___ bad mood ___ _____ _____ _____ ___ pain.

- Once ________ realized ____ ________ _____ ________,
- ____ challenge _____ _____ __ _____ _______ communicate.
- ________ _____ impossible __ ____ Ron's hand move,
- ____ specially trained assistant _______ ______ __
- ____ ______ translates ________ micro movements ______ ______

  _____ __ keyboard.
- __ ___ _____ ________ _____ _____ _____ _____ discovered ____

  _____ really wrong _____ me, Ron ________.
- __ _____ ___ ________ ________.
- ____ Dr. Laureys, Ron's story _____ ______ thrilling ____ alarming.
- __ __ _____ __ patients diagnosed vegetative __ _________ ______

  means ______ ______ support ________ legally __ switched ___,
- Dr. Laurey _____ 40% __ _____ ________ ________ __ consciousness.
- "__ ________, __ ________, 40% ______ unacceptable! _____ ______

  __ do better

  ____ _____ ______ _____ accurate ______ _____ objective

  measurements ______

  ______ __ ________ __ ________ ____ ______ _____ ____ ____

  patients."
- __ _____ ______ __ ______ _____ brought Ron Houben __ ____

  _____ ______ ______ __ ______.

- Elizabeth Palmer, CBS News, London.
- _____ __ __ scientific milestone, 150 _____ _____ ______, Charles Darwin's ____ ____ _____ __ species _____ published.
- Marking ____ anniversary __ ______ edition _____ _____ ____ _______ _____ $170,000 __ Christie's auction house __ London.
- ______ particular ______ _____ __________ ____ ____ _____ __ __ Oxford professor's bathroom _____ ____ _____ __ _____ discovered ___ _____.

15

Reigning genius Stephen Hawking's interview

And remarkable. The reigning genius Stephen Hawking on his children and the quest that disease cannot curb.
From ABC News, this is ABC World News with Diane Sawyer.
We had a rare chance to catch up with a man whose mind has been ranked with Einstein and Newton.
Stephen Hawking was honored recently at the world's science festival.
His daily life is constricted by Lou Gehrig's disease.

68-year-old Stephen Hawking, physicist, father, philosopher.

Body so disabled by ALS, he has the control of only one muscle in his right cheek which twitches to become his voice.

His daughter, lucy. “Every single word comes from a movement of a cheek muscle.

A very tiny specific muscular movement.

That requires extreme dedication and commitment.”

Each twitch moves a cursor to a letter or number, a preexisting word.

And because he can only type one to two words a minute, we told him what we wanted to ask beforehand.

His words are then read by computerized voice.

He was 21 years old, a university student, when suddenly he started falling for no apparent reason with the diagnosis, ALS, Lou Gehrig's disease, he said he felt he faced an execution.

But then racing against the clock, he turned to his work.

He married twice, had three children, and outlived the prognosis by 43 years treating every single day as a chance to ask a new question.

If the universe gave you a giant gift tomorrow, an answer, what's the answer you most want?

“I want to know why the universe exists.”

Hawking has said he believes in the creative majesty of scientific law, not a personal God for humans.

“When you look at the vast size of the universe, and how insignificant and accidental human life is in it, that seems most implausible.”

Recently in a discovery channel series, he made news saying somewhere in the

universe, there must be other living things.
He even dreamed of their possible shapes and sizes, but warned they may not be so friendly.

And then in 2007, he got to experience the wonder of flying in space himself in a zero gravity airplane.
Finally, his own body, no burden, then back to earth.
And his three children, three grandchildren who say he may have taught the world about black holes and gravity, but he taught them about daily courage and infinite kindness.
And then what do you say to your children?
What is the best fatherly advice that you give them?

"Here are the most important pieces of advice that I've passed on to my children.
One, remember to look up at the stars and not down at your feet.
Two, never give up work.
Work gives you meaning and purpose and life is empty without it."
That's beautiful advice.
"Three, if you are lucky enough to find love, remember it is rare, and don't throw it away."
Lucky children to have you.

Words and Idioms

- curb 억제하다/ 억제

  - He needs to learn to **curb** his temper.
    그는 성질을 죽이는 법을 배워야 한다.

- constricted 압축하다 / 제약

  - Her throat **constricted** and she swallowed hard.
    그녀는 목이 조이는 듯 하고 침을 삼키기가 힘들었다.

- twitches 씰룩 거리다 / 홱 잡아당기다

  - Her lips **twitched** with amusement.
    그녀는 재미있어서 입술이 씰룩거렸다.

- dedication and commitment 전념과 노력

- prognosis 예측

  - The **prognosis** is for more people to work part-time in the future.
    앞으로는 더 많은 사람들이 파트타임으로 일할 것으로 예상된다.

- insignificant 하찮은

  - He made her feel **insignificant** and stupid.
    그는 그녀에게 하찮고 바보 같다는 기분이 들게 했다.

- implausible 믿기 어려운

  - It was all highly **implausible**.
    그것은 모두 대단히 믿기 어려웠다.

- infinite 무한한

  - We had a rare chance to catch up with a man **whose** mind has been ranked with Einstein and Newton.
    * catch up with는 '~을 따라잡다'로 그 동안 듣지 못한 소식을 듣는다 의미로 쓰였다.

* 소유격 관계대명사 **whose(=and his)**는 앞에 오는 명사 a man을 수식한다.

– But then **racing** against the clock, he turned to his work.

* race against the clock 은 '시계와 경주하다'는 의미로 시간이 없어 촉박한 상태를 뜻한다.
즉, '한시 바삐'라는 내용을 내포한다.

번역 뛰어난 천재 스티븐 호킹박사 인터뷰

놀랍습니다. 자녀들과 질병도 억제하지 못한 질문에 관한 지배적인 천재과학자인 스티븐 호킹 박사 소식입니다.
ABC 뉴스 국제부에서 다이앤 소여 앵커가 ABC 월드 뉴스를 전해드립니다.
저희는 드물게 아인슈타인과 뉴튼과 같은 과학자와 같은 등급의 두뇌를 가진 사람의 그간 소식을 들을 기회를 얻게 됐습니다.
최근 월드 사이언스 페스티벌(World Science Festival)에서 스티븐 호킹 박사에게 존경을 표했습니다. 그의 일상생활은 루게릭병으로 많은 제약을 받습니다.

스티븐 호킹(68) 박사는 물리학자이고 아버지며 철학자입니다.
루게릭병(ALS)으로 극심한 장애를 겪고 있기 때문에 박사는 의견을 말하기 위해 씰룩 거릴 수 있는 오른쪽 볼의 근육만으로 몸을 제어 합니다.
딸 루시에 따르면 '볼 근육 움직임을 통해 모든 단어가 표현된다'고 합니다.
"상당히 작은 특정한 근육의 움직임입니다. 이를 위해 엄청난 노력과 헌신이 필요합니다.
씰룩 거리는 움직임은 제각각 문자 또는 숫자, 기존의 단어가 쓰여진 커서를 움직입니다.
박사는 타자로 일분에 한두 단어만 쓸 수 있기 때문에 우리가 질문하고 싶은 내용을 앞서 박사에게 알려줬습니다. 그런 다음 박사의 말은 컴퓨터 목소리로 읽혀졌습니다.

그는 21살이 되던 해 대학생이었습니다. 그 때 갑자기 루게릭병으로 뚜렷한 이유 없이 넘어지기 시작했습니다. 그는 사형선고를 받은 느낌이었다고 전했습니다.
하지만 한시 바삐 그는 자신의 일로 돌아왔습니다. 두 번의 결혼 뒤 세 명의 자녀를 얻었고 하루하루를 새로운 질문에 답을 찾는 기회로 삼으면서 43살까지 살 것이라는 예측을 뛰어넘어 더 오래 살았습니다.
만일 우주가 내일 어마어마한 선물을 박사님에게 준다면 가장 얻고 싶은 답은 무엇입니까?
"왜 우주가 존재하는지 그 이유를 알고 싶습니다."

호킹 박사는 인간을 위한 인격적인 신이 아닌 과학적 법칙의 창조적인 장엄함을 믿는다고 밝혔습니다.
"방대한 우주를 본다면 그 우주 안에서 인간의 삶이 얼마나 미약하고 우연한 것인지를 생각하면 그런 관계는 받아들이기 어려울 것입니다."
최근 〈디스커퍼리 채널〉 시리즈에서 호킹 박사는 우주 어딘가에 다른 생명체들의 존재설을 밝혀 뉴스거리를 만들었습니다.
심지어 외계 생명체의 형태 및 크기를 상상하기까지 했지만, 이들이 우호적이지 않을 수도 있다는 점을 경고했습니다.

2007년, 〈제로 그래비티〉 비행기를 타고 우주 공간을 비행하는 놀라운 경험을 했습니다.
마침내 몸에는 어떠한 무리도 없이 지구로 돌아왔습니다.

세 명의 자녀와 세 명의 손자들은 그가 세상에 블랙홀과 중력을 가르쳤을지 모르지만
자신들에게는 매일 용기와 한없는 친절함을 교육시켰다고 전합니다.
아이들에게 어떤 말씀을 하시나요?
아버지로서 자녀들에게 해 줬던 최고의 조언은 무엇인가요?
"제 아이들에게 했던 가장 중요한 조언들이 여기 몇 가지 있습니다.
첫째, 발아래를 내려다보지 말고 눈을 들어 별을 보거라.
둘째, 지금 하는 일을 절대 포기하지 말라. 일은 너희들에게 의미와 목적을 준다. 인생은 그것 없이는 공허하단다. 아름다운 충고입니다.
셋째, 사랑을 찾았다면, 사랑은 드문 기회라는 것을 기억하고 버리지 말거라."
박사님과 같은 아버지를 두어 행운을 얻은 자녀들이군요.

Dictation

- _____ remarkable. _____ reigning genius Stephen Hawking
- ___ ______ children _____ _____ quest ______ disease cannot curb .
- ______ ABC News, ______ ___ ABC World News ______ Diane Sawyer.
- ____ _____ ___ rare chance ___ catch ____ ______ ___ man whose mind _____ ______ ranked ______ Einstein _____ Newton.
- Stephen Hawking _____ honored recently ___ _____ world's science festival.
- ______ daily life ___ constricted ___ Lou Gehrig's disease.
- 68-________-________ Stephen Hawking, physicist, father, philosopher.

- Body ____ disabled ___ ALS, ____ _____ _____ control ___ only ____ muscle ___ ______ right cheek
- which twitches ___ become ______ voice.
- ______ daughter, lucy. "_______ single word comes ______ ___ movement ___ ___ cheek muscle.
- ___ very tiny specific muscular movement.
- ______ requires extreme dedication _____ commitment ."
- Each twitch moves ___ cursor ___ ___ letter ____ number, ___ preexisting word.
- _____ because ____ ____ only type ____ ___ ______ words ___ minute, ____ told ______ _______ ____ wanted ___ ask beforehand.
- ______ words _____ then read ___ computerized voice.
- ____ _____ 21 years _______, ___ university student, ______ suddenly ____ started falling _____ no apparent reason
- ______ _____ diagnosis, ALS, Lou Gehrig's disease, ____ _______ ____ felt ____ faced ___ execution.
- _____ then racing against _____ clock, ____ turned ___ ______ work.
- ____ married twice, _____ three children, _____ outlived _____ prognosis ___ 43 years
- treating _______ single day _____ ___ chance ___ ask ___ new question.
- _____ _____ universe gave ____ ___ giant gift tomorrow, ___ answer,

__________ ____ answer ___ ______ want?

- "___ want ___ ______ ______ ____ universe exists."
- Hawking ____ ______ ___ believes ___ ____ creative majesty ___ scientific law, not ___ personal god ____ humans.
- "______ ___ ______ ___ ____ vast ______ ___ ____ universe, ____ ____ insignificant ____ accidental human life ___ ___ ___,
- ______ seems ______ implausible ."
- Recently ___ ___ discovery channel series, ___ ______ news saying somewhere ___ ____ universe, _______ must ___ other living things.
- ___ ______ dreamed ___ _______ possible shapes ____ sizes,
- ____ warned ______ _____ not ___ ___ friendly.
- ____ then ___ 2007, ___ got ___ experience ____ wonder ___ flying ___ space himself ___ ___ zero gravity airplane.
- Finally, ______ ___ body, no burden, then back ___ earth.
- ____ ______ three children, three grandchildren ____ ____
- ___ _____ ______ taught ____ world ______ black holes ____ gravity,
- ____ ___ taught ______ ______ daily c______age ____ infinite kindness.
- ____ then ______ ___ ___ ____ ___ ______ children?
- ______ ___ ____ best fatherly advice ______ ___ give ______?

- "_______ ____ _____ _______ important pieces ___ advice _______ ___'ve passed ___ ___ ____ children.
- ___, remember ___ _______ ____ ___ _____ stars _____ not _______ ___ _______ feet.
- ______, never give ____ work.
- Work gives ____ meaning _____ purpose _____ life ___ empty without ___."
- __________ beautiful advice.
- "Three, _____ ____ _____ lucky enough ___ find ______, remember ___ ___ rare, _____ don't throw ___ _______." Lucky children ___ _______ ____.

16

Superbugs appear

Superbugs. Deadly drug resistant bacteria creating a dangerous new and global threat.

Dr. Richard Besser is here with what you need to know.

From ABC News headquarters, this is ABC World news with Diane Sawyer.

From scientists today, they discovered a new gene.

They can turn any bacteria and one of the superbugs that's hard to kill with antibiotics.

It's been turning up in hospitals here and overseas.

And the doctors who found the gene warned that it could soon become a worldwide public health problem.

Our senior medical editor Dr. Richard Besser has more on the threat.

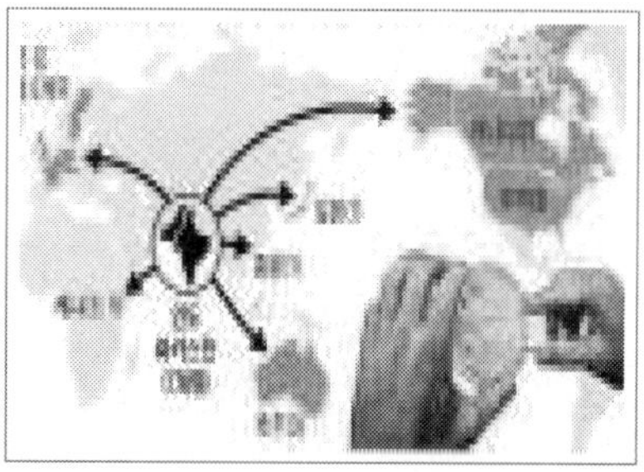

A new study in Lancet infectious diseases documents the spread of a gene called NDM-1.

They can turn almost any type of bacteria into a powerful super bug.

Even the strongest antibiotics are unable to treat these infections.

The drug resistance is spread by Plasmids, genetic material that can hop from organism to organism which are then freed to reproduce and share the resistance with other bacteria.

Originally found in India and Pakistan, the gene has now been seen in the United States, the United Kingdom, Netherlands, Australia and Canada.

It's believed the worldwide spread is linked to tourists who received medical care in India and Pakistan.

"The three cases that were reported in June in the United States all retraceable to people who have been in India."

Tackling this problem were required not only preventing these infections, but also creating new antibiotics.

The problem is few new antibiotics are being produced.

"We are not developing new drugs. And a few drugs in development are not going to handle our problem.

We have a real crisis in antibiotic development right now."

Words and Idioms

- antibiotic 항생의, 항생물질
- gene 유전자
- drug resistance 약제 내성
- retraceable 왔던 길을 다시 돌아가는
- infection 전염

– Superbugs. **Deadly** drug resistant bacteria creating a dangerous new and global threat.

* '**deadly**'는 '치명적인'이라는 의미로 '죽음에 이르게 할 정도'라는 것을 내포하고 있다.

– Tackling this problem were required **not only preventing** these infections, **but also creating** new antibiotics.

* 'not only A, but (also) B' 구문은 'A 뿐만 아니라 B 도'라는 의미로 A와 B의 형태는 같아야 한다. 동인어구로 'merely, simply, alone, just A, but (also) B'가 있다.

번역 슈퍼박테리아 출현

슈퍼버그는 치명적인 약제내성박테리아로 전 세계에 새로운 위협이 되고 있습니다.

리차드 베서박사가 이 자리에서 우리가 무엇을 알아야 하는지 알려주겠습니다.

ABC 방송국 다이너 소어의 ABC 월드뉴스입니다.
오늘 과학자들은 새로운 유전자를 발견했습니다.
이들은 어떤 박테리아도 항생제에 저항력이 있는 슈퍼버그로 바꿀 수 있습니다.
이것은 전 세계의 병원에서 등장하고 있습니다.
의사들은 자신들이 발견했던 유전자가 곧 전 세계적으로 공중보건문제를 야기할 것이라고 경고했습니다.
의학부문 선임편입위원 리차드 베서박사가 자세한 소식을 전하겠습니다.

영국의학지 '란센트 전염병'의 새로운 연구에서 NDM-1이라 불리는 유전자의 확산을 다루었습니다.
이들은 거의 어떠한 박테리아도 강력한 슈퍼버그로 바꿀 수 있습니다.
심지어 가장 강력한 항생제도 이 전염병을 치료할 수 없습니다.
이러한 약제내성력은 플라스미드에 의해 퍼집니다.
유전물질로서 유기체들 사이에서 이동이 가능합니다.
이동 후 복제되어 다른 박테리아와 약제 내성력을 공유합니다.
이 유전자는 인도와 파키스탄에서 처음 발견되었습니다.
하지만 현재 미국, 영국, 네델란드, 호주, 캐나다에서도 발견되고 있습니다.

이러한 전 세계적인 확산은 인도와 파키스탄에서 의료관광을 다녀온 환자들 때문이라고 여겨집니다.
"미국에서 6월에 보고되었던 3건의 감염사례 모두 인도에 방문했던 사람들이었습니다."
이 문제를 해결하기 위해서는 전염병 예방관리뿐만 아니라 새로운 항생제도 만들어야 합니다. 문제는 새로운 항생제가 거의 개발되고 있지 않다는 것입니다.
"새로운 약이 개발되고 있지 않고 있어요. 또한 개발 중인 몇 개의 약도 이 문제를 해결해주지는 못할 것입니다."
우리는 현재 항생제 개발에 대한 실질적인 위기에 봉착하고 있습니다.

Dictation

- Superbugs. Deadly drug resistant bacteria creating ___ dangerous new _____ global threat.
- Dr. Richard Besser ___ ______ ______ ______ ___ need ___ know.
- ______ ABC News headquarters, ______ ___ ABC World news _____ Diane Sawyer.
- ______ scientists today, ______ discovered ___ new gene.
- ______ ___ _______ any bacteria _____ one ___ _____ superbugs ___________ hard ___ kill _____ antibiotics.
- _____ ______ turning ____ ___ hospitals ______ _____ overseas.
- _____ _____ doctors _____ found _____ gene warned ______ ___ ______ soon ______ ___ worldwide public health problem.
- ____ senior medical editor Dr. Richard Besser ____ ______ ___ _____ threat.
- ___ new study ___ Lancet infectious diseases documents _____ spread ___ ___ gene called NDM-1.
- ______ ____ _______ almost any type ___ bacteria _______ ___ powerful super bug.
- Even _____ strongest antibiotics _____ unable ___ treat ______ infections.
- _____ drug resistance ___ spread ___ Plasmids ,

- genetic material ______ ____ hop ______ organism ___ organism
- _____ _____ ______ freed ___ reproduce _____ share _____ resistance _____ _____ bacteria.
- Originally found ___ India _____ Pakistan,
- _____ gene ____ now _____ ______ ___ _____ United States, _____ United Kingdom, Netherlands, Australia _____ Canada.
- _____ believed _____ worldwide spread ___ linked ___ tourists _____ received medical care ___ India _____ Pakistan.
- "_____ _____ cases ______ ______ reported ___ June ___ _____ United States ____ retraceable ___ people _____ ______ _____ ___ India."
- Tackling ______ problem ______ required not _____ preventing ______ infections,
- ______ _____ creating new antibiotics.
- _____ problem ___ few new antibiotics _____ _____ produced.
- "_____ _____ not developing new drugs. _____ ___ few drugs ___ development _____ not _______ ___ handle ____ problem.
- _____ ______ ___ _____ crisis ___ antibiotic development _____ now."

17

Cyber Army for Teenagers

Uncle Sam wants you?

The government recruits an army of teenagers for homeland security.

From ABC News headquarters, this is ABC World News with Diane Sawyer.

And is it possible that the nation needs more teenagers to preserve homeland security?

The Pentagon has just confirmed for the first time that foreign computer hackers were able to break into so many secret files. It created the most serious breach ever.

And Pierre Thomas has learned one of the surprising ways the US plans to fight back.

Tonight in fact right now, the nation is under attack.
Not from tanks or missiles, but an invisible assault, with the US being hit on all sides.
"We're being scanned millions of times a day.
There are attempted intrusions that happen thousands of times a day."
William Lynn is the 56-year-old deputy secretary of defense.
He's the man who has to worry about those 1,000 hack attempts a day.

Beyond the millions spent fighting this new war, the government is increasingly pinning its hopes on some unlikely recruits.
Meet the baby-faced warriors, the green berets in this new age war.
America needs an estimated 20,000 to 30,000 young people skilled in hacking.
A national competition was recently launched aimed at finding them.
The targets, teenagers, some as young as 16.

Michael Coppola won the first hacking competition by infiltrating the competition's computers and upping his score.
"I'm told you got skills?"
"What can I say? The young people have the interest in this technology. They have the passion."
"Have they already started to try to recruit you?"
"The navy, actually. They welcome to recruit me. But I didn't make a decision."
"Have you ever snuck around some systems that you weren't supposed to be in?"
"No comment."
Already hackers have tried to steal battlefield war plans, access secret weapons' designs.

In what is now being called the worst breach of military computers ever, hackers were able to compromise classified information from the command overseeing US war operations in Iraq and Afghanistan.

"It was an important moment, it……… I think changed our understanding of the threat."
The US wants to act fast.
The Chinese have already amassed a force of young hackers.
And some, at this very moment, are preparing.
The war force for the 21st century.
Pierre Thomas, ABC News, Washington.

Words and Idioms

- breach 단절 파괴 위반
- a breach of contract/copyright/warranty 계약/저작권/보증 위반
- compromise 타협/ 타협하다 / 위태롭게 하다
  - After lengthy talks the two sides finally reached a **compromise**.
    오랜 회담 끝에 양측이 마침내 타협에 이르렀다.
- amassed 축적하다 / 모이다
  - He **amassed** a fortune from silver mining.
    그는 은광 업으로 큰 재산을 모았다.

• intrusion (무단)침입/ 마음대로 들어감

- They claim the noise from the new airport is an **intrusion** on their lives.
그들은 새 공항에서 들리는 소음이 그들의 생활을 침해한다고 주장한다.

• infiltrate 잠입하다 / 침투하다/스며들다

- The headquarters had been **infiltrated** by enemy spies.
사령부에 적의 스파이들이 침투했었다.

• assault 습격/ 습격하다

- An **assault** on the capital was launched in the early hours of the morning.
그 수도에 대한 공격은 이른 새벽에 감행되었다.

- Uncle Sam wants you?
* **Uncle Sam**은 미국정부를 의미한다.

- the government is increasingly **pinning its hopes on** some unlikely recruits
* **pin one's hope on**은 "~에 희망을 걸다"라는 의미다.

번역 십대 사이버 용병

미국정부가 여러분을 원할까요?

미 정부는 국가안보를 위해 소년병을 모집하고 있습니다.

다이너 소어의 ABC 뉴스입니다.

국가가 자국안보를 위해 많은 십대들이 필요하다는 것이 있을 수 있는 얘기일까요?

국방부가 최초로 공식화한 것은 외국의 컴퓨터해커들이 많은 기밀문서에 접

근할 수 있었다는 것입니다. 이는 안보의 심각한 파괴였습니다.
피에르 토마스기자가 놀라운 미국의 반격계획에 대해 보도하겠습니다.

사실 바로 오늘밤에도 미국은 공격을 당하고 있습니다.
탱크나 미사일 따위의 공격이 아닙니다. 미국은 도처에서 보이지 않는 공격을 받고 있습니다.
"우리를 노리는 건수도 하루에 수백만 건이나 됩니다. 그리고 공격시도도 하루에 수천 건 있습니다." 윌리엄 린은 56세의 국방부 차관입니다.
그는 하루에 이러한 천 건의 해커공격을 우려해야 하는 사람입니다.

수백만 명이 이러한 새로운 전쟁과 싸우는 차원을 넘어서 미 정부는 독특한 고용방식에 점점 더 희망을 걸고 있습니다.
앳된 얼굴의 용사들을 만나보십시오. 새로운 전쟁의 특전부대원들입니다.
미국은 해킹능력을 갖춘 대략 20,000~30,000명의 청소년을 필요로 합니다.
정부는 이들은 찾기 위해 최근에 경연대회를 열었습니다.
타깃은 십대청소년이며 16살 청소년도 있습니다.

마이클 쿠폴라는 이 대회의 첫 번째 우승자입니다.
마이클은 대회장 컴퓨터에 침입하여 자신의 점수를 올렸습니다.
"해킹기술이 있다고 들었는데요?"
"뭐라고 말해야 할지… 십대들은 이 기술에 관심을 가지고 있고 열정도 가지고 있습니다."
"이미 채용문의가 시작되었죠?"
"사실 해군에서 연락이 왔어요. 저를 기꺼이 채용한다고 하더군요. 하지만 결정은 내리지 못했어요."
"들어가서는 안 될 일부 시스템을 기웃거린 적은 있었나요?", "답변은 하지 않겠습니다."

해커들은 이미 전쟁터의 군사작전과 기밀 무기 디자인 정보를 빼내려고 했었습니다.
현재 최악의 군사컴퓨터시스템 침범이라 불리는 상황에서 해커들이 위태롭게 할 수 있었던 기밀정보는 이라크와 아프가니스탄의 미 군사작전을 감독하는 사령부에서 나온 것입니다.

"중요한 시점이었습니다. 이것으로 인해 위협에 대한 생각이 바뀌게 된 것 같습니다."
미국은 빠르게 대처하기를 원합니다.
중국은 이미 젊은 해커군단을 축적해왔습니다.
그리고 바로 지금 일부 국가가 준비하고 있는 것은 21세기를 위한 전력입니다.
워싱턴에서 ABC 뉴스 피에르 토마스였습니다.

Dictation

- ____ ____ _____ _____
- _____ _______ _______ an army of teenagers _____ ________ ________.
- From ABC News headquarters, this is ABC World News with Diane Sawyer.
- _____ ______ _____ _______ that the nation ______ _____ _____ __ _______ ______ _______?
- The Pentagon has______ ______ ______ ____ ______ _____ that

foreign computer hackers

______ ______ ____ ______ ______ so many secret files. __ ______

_____ ________ ______ ________.

- And Pierre Thomas ______ ______ ______ ____ ____ ______ _____

  the US plans ____ ______ _______.

- _______ ____ ______ ______ _____, _____ ______ ____ ____

  _______.

- Not from tanks or missiles, ____ _____ ______ _______, ____ _____

  _____ ______ _____ ______ ____ ________.

- We're ______ ________ _________ ______ _______ ___ ______.

- There are attempted intrusions that _________ _______ ______ ___ _

  _____."

- William Lynn___ _______ _______ ____ ______ _____ _________.

- He's the man ______ ______ ____ _____ ______ ______ ______

  ______ ______ ____ ______.

- ______ _____ ______ _______ ______ _____ ___ _____,

  the government is increasingly pinning _____ ___________ _______

  ______ ________.

- ______ ____ ______ ______, the green berets in this new age war.

- America needs ____ _________ _______ ______ _______ young people

  ______ ______ _________.

- ____ ____ ____ ____ ____ ____ ____ at finding them.
- ____ ____, ____, some as young as 16.
  Michael Coppola ____ ____ ____ ____ ____ ____ ____ the competition's computers ____ ____ ____ ____.
- “____ ____ ____ ____ ____?”
- “What can I say? ____ ____ ____ ____ ____ ____ ____ ____ ____. They have the passion.”
- “____ ____ ____ ____ ____ ____ ____ ____ ____?”
- “The navy, actually. ____ ____ ____ ____ ____. ____ ____ ____ ____ ____ ____.”
- “Have you ever ____ ____ ____ ____ ____ ____ ____ ____ ____ ____ ____” “____ ____.”
- Already hackers have tried to steal battlefield war plans, ____ ____ ____ ____.
- ____ ____ ____ ____ ____ ____ ____ ____ ____ ____ military computers ever hackers ____ ____ ____ ____ ____ information ____ ____ ____ overseeing US war operations in Iraq and Afghanistan.
- “____ ____ ____ ____ ____, it……… I think changed our understanding of the threat.”,
- ____ ____ ____ ____ ____ ____.

- The Chinese ______ ______ __________ a force of young hackers.
- And some, ___ ______ _______ _______,______ _________.
- ______ ______ _______ _______ ______ _______ _________.

Pierre Thomas, ABC News, Washington.

18

The secret of longevity

And living longer. News about living past 100 and thriving.

From ABC News headquarters, this is ABC World News with Diane Sawyer.

We all know about those people who live well past 100, vibrant, thriving.

Is it some special food or some rule they live by or something scientists reported today.

Here's Sherrill Alfonzi.

Meet Aggie Fadden, believe it or not, she's just weeks away from celebrating her 105 th birthday.

So we asked her what is the secret to her long life?

“Drink good booze, drink good booze! That's kept you well preserved?”, “Right.

Right."

If it sounds crazy, consider the latest science on the subject.

Researchers now say living into your hundreds may have less to do with what you eat or drink, and more to do with the combination of a series of very specific genes.

Those genes can actually predict longevity.

Almost all the centenarians they studied have that combination.

"I'm….be 111. Wonderful. I've never been that old before"

Benie Madigan thinks her genes did play a key role in her long life.

Specifically the fact that she never passed those genes on.

"No kids, no stress, no strain."

And scientists say those longevity genes could also protect you from serious disease.

Aggie told us she's only had one serious health problem in all her years. A benign tumor.

"And what did the doctor tell you? What was his advice to you?"

"When he discharged me, he said, Aggie, you must drink three Miller Highlite a day."

So Aggie has enjoyed three beers and a shot of scotch every day for almost 70 years with an unquenchable thirst for more.

Sherrill Alfonzi, ABC News, Angerwood, New Jersey.

Could beer be the fountain of youth? I don't know.

Have a great night and we'll see you here again tomorrow. Bye.

Words and Idioms

- vibrant 활기찬 / 강렬한
  - It was those **vibrant** eyes of him that had attracted her.
    그녀를 단번에 반하게 했던 것은 바로 그의 빛나는 눈동자였다.
- centenarians 100 세 이상 장수자
  - There are many more **centenarians** now than there were 30 years ago.
    지금은 30년전보다 백살까지 사는 사람들이 더욱 많아졌다.
- benign tumor 양성종양
  - Once a **benign tumor** is removed, it does not return.
    양성종양은 한번 제거되고 나면, 다시 생기지 않는다.
- discharged 퇴원시키다
  - She had **discharged** herself against medical advice.
    그녀는 의사의 충고를 따르지 않고 퇴원을 했었다.
- unquenchable 채울 수 없는
  - He is a man with an **unquenchable** thirst for knowledge.
    그는 지식에 대한 갈증이 많은 사람이다.
  - Researchers now say living into your hundreds may **have less to do with** what you eat or drink, and more to do with the combination of a series of very specific genes.
    * **have something(nothing) to do with**는 '~와 관계가 있다(없다)'로 여기에서는 그 정도를 나타내기 위해 less와 more를 사용했다.
  - Specifically the fact that she never passed those genes on.
    * pass on은 '~에게 넘겨주다(전달하다)'는 의미이다.

번역 장수의 비결

장수할 수 있습니다. 100세를 넘는 삶과 번영에 관한 소식입니다.

ABC 뉴스 국제부에서 다이앤 소여 앵커가 ABC 월드 뉴스를 전해드립니다.

100세를 거뜬히 넘기고도 활발하고 건강하게 잘 사고 있는 이들에 대한 이야기를 잘 알고 있습니다.

특별한 음식이나 그들이 지키는 어떤 규칙 같은 것이 있는 걸까요?

과학자들이 오늘 특별한 소식을 보고했습니다.

셔릴 알폰지 기자가 보도합니다.

애기 패든 씨를 만나보겠습니다. 믿거나 말거나 그녀는 105번째 생일을 몇 주 남겨 놓고 있습니다.

그녀에게 장수 비결이 뭔지 질문했습니다.

"좋은 술을 마십니다.", "좋은 술을 드시는군요! 그것이 건강을 잘 지켜줬나요?", "맞습니다."

말도 안 되는 소리 같지만 이 주제에 대한 최근 연구 결과를 생각해 보시기 바랍니다.

연구진에 따르면 100세 이상 사는 것은 당신이 먹는 음식이나 음료와는 연관성이 적을 수도 있습니다.

오히려 일련의 특정한 유전자 조합과 더 관련이 있을 수 있습니다.

유전자가 실질적으로 장수를 예측할 수 있습니다.

연구진이 연구한 100세 이상 장수한 사람들은 거의 그러한 조합을 보였습니다.

"저는 … 111세가 됩니다. 놀랍죠. 전에는 그렇게 늙지 않았답니다."

베니 매디건 씨는 자신의 유전자가 장수에 중요한 역할을 했다고 생각합니다.

특히 그 유전자를 (후손에게) 전달해 주지 않았다는 사실에 주목합니다.

"자녀도 없고, 스트레스와 피곤도 없습니다."

과학자들은 장수 유전자는 심각한 질병으로부터 그런 사람을 보호할 수 있습니다.

애기 씨는 평생에 단 한번 심각한 건강 문제를 앓았습니다. 바로 양성종양입니다.

"의사가 무슨 말을 하던가요? 어떤 조언을 했죠?"

"의사가 저를 퇴원시킬 때 '애기, 하루에 밀러 하이라이트를 세 캔 마셔야 됩니다!'라고 제게 말했어요."

그래서 애기 씨는 채워지지 않는 갈증으로 맥주 세 캔과 스카치 한 잔을 70년간 매일 마셨습니다.

뉴저지 앵글우드에서 ABC 뉴스, 셔릴 알폰지 기자였습니다.

맥주가 젊음의 원천이 될까요? 저는 잘 모르겠군요.

좋은 밤 되시기 바랍니다. 저희는 내일 다시 뵙겠습니다.

Dictation

- _____ living longer. News ________ living past 100 _____ thriving.
- _______ ABC News headquarters, _______ ___ ABC World News _______ Diane Sawyer.
- ____ _______ ________ ________ _________ people _____ live well past 100, vibrant , thriving.
- ___ ___ some special _______ ____ some rule _______ live ___ ____ something scientists reported today.

- __________ Sherrill Alfonzi.
- Meet Aggie Fadden, believe __ ___ not, __________ just weeks ______ ______ celebrating _____ 105 th birthday.
- ___ ___ asked _____ _______ __ ____ secret __ _____ long life?
- "Drink good booze, drink good booze! _________ kept ___ well preserved?", "Right. Right."
- ___ __ sounds crazy, consider ____ latest science __ ____ subject.
- Researchers ______ _____ living ______ ______ hundreds _____ ______ less __ ___ ______ _______ ___ ___ ___ drink,
- ____ ______ __ ___ ______ ____ combination __ __ series __ very specific genes.
- ________ genes ___ actually predict longevity.
- Almost ______ ____ centenarians ______ studied ______ ______ combination.
- "______….___ 111. Wonderful. __'ve never ______ ______ _______ before "
- Benie Madigan thinks _____ genes did play __ key role __ _____ long life.
- Specifically ____ _______ ______ ___ never passed ________ genes ___.
- "No kids, no stress, no strain."
- ____ scientists ____ ________ longevity genes _________ also protect

____ ______ serious disease.

- Aggie told us __________ only ____ ___ serious health problem ___ ______ _____ years. ___ benign tumor .
- "_____ _______ did ____ doctor tell ___? _______ ____ ______ advice ___ ___?"
- "______ ___ discharged me, ___ _______, Aggie, ___ must drink three Miller Highlite ___ day."
- ___ Aggie ____ enjoyed three beers ____ ___ shot ___ scotch _______ day ____ almost 70 years
- ______ ___ unquenchable thirst ____ ______.
- Sherrill Alfonzi, ABC News, Angerwood, New Jersey.
- _________ beer ___ _____ fountain ___ youth? ___ don't _______.
- ______ ___ ______ night ____ _______ ___ ___ _______ again tomorrow. Bye.

19

The USA the greatest oil gusher

Tonight, can anything stop it?

That massive oil spill is closing in on the Gulf Coast threatening to destroy fragile marshland, wildlife and the fishing industry.

From CBS News world headquarters in New York.

As Mark reported, all of this began with an explosion on an oil rig.

The cause of that explosion is still unknown, but tonight some experts say it should never have led to a disaster of this magnitude.

And Ben Tracy tells us, they're blaming the federal government for lax safety standards.

The black cloud in the Gulf of Mexico is growing by the minute with up to 5,000 barrels of oil pouring into the water, that's 210,000 gallons each day, enough to fill an Olympic-sized swimming pool every four days.
“This could be one of the world's greatest nightmare scenarios of an oil gusher.”
Today Senator Bill Nelson sent the president a letter reminding him that in 2000, the Interior Department insisted oil companies have reliable backup systems in the event of a rig blowout. By 2003, the plan was scrapped.

Here's how it could have helped.
When an oil rig fails and starts leaking, a valve deep under the water where the drill pipe meets the ocean floor is supposed to choke off the flow of oil, either it wasn't activated or didn't work, possibly because of the explosion.
But there is another line of defense this oil platform did not have, a so-called acoustic switch.
It can be activated by a remote control, sending acoustic pulses through the water to trigger the blowout preventer if the rig is damaged or evacuated.

Acoustic switches are now used in Norway and Brazil after those oil-producing countries suffered spills.
The US considered requiring them, but drilling companies questioned the $500,000 cost and whether the devices even work.
The spill in the Gulf comes at a time when President Obama is calling for a major expansion of offshore drilling.
Today, Florida's Senator Nelson said not so fast, proposing legislation to temporarily halt the president's plan.
The administration now says everything is back on the table as that black cloud

in the Gulf continues to spread.

Ben Tracy, CBS News, Los Angeles.

Words and Idioms

- marshland 습지대
  - Bogs and **marshland** make up the shores of Alpine Lake in Europe.
    늪지와 소택지들이 유럽의 알파인 호수 주변을 이루고 있다.
- oil rig 석유굴착장치
- gusher 분유정
- choke off 제한하다 /(비명을) 지르지 못하게 하다
- acoustic 음향
  - A Study on the **Acoustic** Characteristics of Outdoor Performance Hall
    야외공연장의 음향 특성에 관한 연구
  - **an acoustic instrument** 보청기
  - That massive oil spill is **closing** in on the Gulf Coast threatening to destroy fragile marshland, wildlife and the fishing industry.
    * **close**는 '~으로 막다, 봉하다, 메우다'는 뜻으로 지금도 계속 기름이 유출되는 상황을 나타내므로 현재진행형 [be+ -ing]으로 나타냈다. [threaten to + 동사원형]은 '~할 우려가 있다. ~할 듯하다'는 의미다.

- Today, Florida's Senator Nelson said **not so fast**, proposing legislation to temporarily halt the president's plan.
  * **not so fast**는 '잠깐, 기다려, 너무 성급히 하지마 등'의 의미가 있다.
- The administration now says everything is back **on the table**.
  * **everything**은 단수 취급하므로 be동사의 형태는 is이다. 여기에서 **on the table**은 숙어로 '검토 중인'을 나타낸다.

번역 미 사상최대 원유누출 재앙

오늘 저녁, 무엇인가 원유 유출을 막을 수 있을까요?
이 막대한 기름 유출은 걸프 연안을 메우고 있으며 취약한 습지대, 야생 및 어업을 파괴시킬 우려가 있습니다.
뉴욕의 CBS 뉴스 국제부에서 보도합니다.
마크 기자가 보도했듯 이 모든 사건은 석유시추시설이 폭발되면서 시작됐습니다.
폭발 원인은 아직도 확인되지 않았습니다.
하지만 오늘 저녁, 몇몇 전문가에 따르면 본 사건이 이 정도 재앙으로 이어지지 않았어야 한다고 합니다.
그들은 느슨한 안전기준에 대해 연방정부를 비난하고 있습니다. 벤 트레이시 기자가 전합니다.

멕시코 만에 검은 구름(기름 띠) 이 시시각각 증가하고 있고, 최대 5,000배럴의 기름이 물속으로 쏟아지고 있습니다. 이는 매일 21만 갤론에 해당하는 양으로 4일마다 올림픽 경기장 수영장 크기를 가득 매울 수준입니다 .
"이번 일은 전 세계 사상 최대 끔찍한 기름 유출 사건 중 하나일 수 있습니다."

오늘, 빌 넬슨 상원의원은 대통령에게 편지를 보냈고, 지난 2000년, 내무부에서 '정유회사들은 시추시설 파열로 인한 기름 유출에 대비해 신뢰할 수 있는 백업 시스템을 갖추어야 한다'고 주장했던 사실을 상기시켰습니다. 2003년경 이 계획은 폐기처분 됐습니다.

여기 도움이 됐을 만한 방법이 있습니다.
석유시추시설이 고장나 기름이 새기 시작할 경우 굴착 파이프와 대양저가 만나는 심해 부분에서 벨브가 기름 흐름을 제한하거나 또는 폭발로 인해 활성화되지 않거나 작동하지 않습니다.
한편, 이 기름 플랫폼에 없던 또 다른 방어책이 있습니다. 흔히 음향 스위치라고 불려지는 장치입니다.
이 장치는 원격제어로 활성화가 가능하며, 석유시추시설이 손상되거나 비었을 때 파열 보호장치를 작동시키기 위해 수중에서 음향 파동을 보냅니다.

음향 스위치는 산유국에서 기름 유출 사건을 겪은 뒤 현재 노르웨이와 브라질에서 사용되고 있습니다.
미국은 이 장치들이 필요하다고 생각했지만, 석유시추기업들은 $500,000에 달하는 비용과 그 장치가 제대로 작동할지에 의문을 품었습니다.
멕시코 만의 기름 유출 사건은 오바마 대통령이 근해 석유시추에 대한 막대한 경비를 요청할 시점에 한 번에 터졌습니다.
오늘, 플로리다주의 넬슨 상원의원은 성급히 판단하지 말 것을 전했고, 일시적으로 대통령의 계획을 일시적으로 중단하는 법률 제정을 제안했습니다.
내각은 멕시코 만의 기름띠가 계속 퍼지고 있기 때문에 모든 것이 검토 중에 있다고 전했습니다.

Dictation

- Tonight, can anything stop it?
- ____________ __________ oil spill is closing in _________ _________ Gulf Coast
- threatening _______ destroy fragile marshland , wildlife and _________ fishing ____________.
- From CBS News world headquarters in New York .
- As Mark reported, all _______ this began with an ____________ _________ an oil __________ .
- _________ cause _______ ____________ ____________ is still ____________,
- but tonight some experts say it should never have ____________ _______ a ____________ this ____________.
- And Ben Tracy tells us, they're ____________ _________ ____________ government _________ ____________ safety standards.
- _________ black cloud in _________ Gulf _______ Mexico is growing by _________ minute
- with up _______ 5,000 barrels _______ oil pouring into _________ water, ____________'s 210,000 gallons each day,
- enough _______ ____________ an Olympic-sized swimming pool every four

days.

- "This could be one ______ ______ world's greatest ______ scenarios ______ an oil gusher ."
- Today Senator Bill Nelson sent ______ president a letter
- ______ him ______ in 2000, ______ ______ Department ______
- oil companies have ______ ______ systems in ______ ______ ______ a ______ ______.
- By 2003, ______ plan was ______.
- Here's how it could have helped.
- When an oil ______ fails and starts ______,
- a ______ deep under ______ water ______ ______ ______ pipe meets ______ ocean floor is supposed ______ ______ ______
- ______ ______ ______ oil,
- either it wasn't ______ or didn't ______, possibly because ______ ______ ______.
- But there is another line ______ defense this oil platform did not have,
- a so-called ______ switch.
- It can be ______ by a ______ control,

- sending __________ pulses through ________ water
- ______ trigger ________ __________ preventer if ________ ________ is damaged or evacuated.
- __________ switches are now used in Norway and Brazil after those oil-producing countries suffered spills.
- ________ US considered requiring them,
- but drilling companies questioned ________ $500,000 cost and whether ________ __________ even __________.
- ________ spill in ________ Gulf comes at a time when President Obama is ________ ________ a major ____________ ______ ____________ drilling.
- Today, Florida 's Senator Nelson said ______ _____ ________,
- proposing ____________ ______ ____________ ____________ ________ president's plan.
- ________ administration now says everything is back ________ ________ ________
- as __________ black cloud in ________ Gulf continues ______ spread.
- Ben Tracy, CBS News, Los Angeles.

20

Compare the education of US and Japan

And finally tonight, president Obama has vowed to improve education in America.
And there are lessons to be learned from some of the countries that are outperforming us right now.
Like Japan where they focus on recruiting the best teachers, then treat them with the reverence and respect they've earned.
Celia Hatton in Tokyo continues our series: Reading, Writing and Reform.

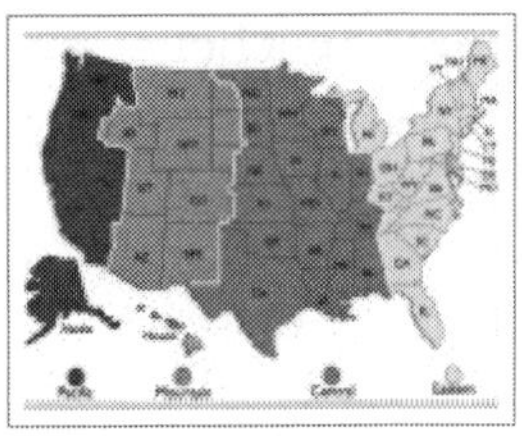
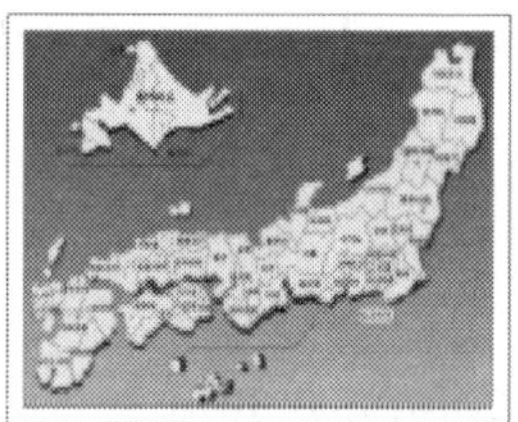

First thing in the morning, Japanese children bow to their teachers.
It's a small gesture that says a lot.

Here, respect is not a song title. It's the backbone, Japan's school system which for decades has topped international rankings while spending the lowest amount on education among developed democracies, 3.3% of Japan's gross domestic product or GDP goes toward schooling compared to 5% in the US.

How do they do so much with so little?
By investing in top-notch teachers.
"Teachers are given a good deal of respect. They're expected to devote their life. The whole system is set up to emphasize the development of teachers."
Retirement comes at 60 for Japanese educators with a salary of more than $62,000 compared to $53,000 in the US.

But in return, teachers are tasked with transforming children into model citizens.
If a student is caught shoplifting, for example, the child's teacher is usually alerted before a parent.
"If our students do something wrong outside the school, we tend to think we should have taught them better."
Inside the classroom, children learn responsibility, changing into slippers at the school's entrance and cleaning the building themselves.
Children take turns dishing out food to their classmates and their teacher and no one takes a bite until everyone is served.

Teachers also have scheduled periods to compare notes.
Their desks are even grouped together in one room.
"I spend 60% of my time with students and 40% with other teachers."
Classes are regularly videotaped, allowing senior teachers to mentor juniors, a

technique that's gaining traction in the US.
And ineffective teachers aren't fired or sidelined here, they're given extensive retraining, explains the president of Japan's teachers' union.
"It's impossible for someone who is incompetent to get through the system."

Despite all this, those all important global test scores have slipped.
Japan topped international math rankings in 2000, but dropped to 6th in 2006, still far ahead the US at number 25.
What hasn't changed in Japan is the value placed on education, best summed up by a Japanese proverb, "better than a thousand days of study is one day with a great teacher."
Celia Hatton, CBS News, Tokyo.

Words and Idioms

- vowed 다짐하다
- outperforming 작업 능력이 ~을 능가하다
- reverence 존경
- respect 경의
- bow 절하다
- backbone 근간

- top-notch 최고의
- devote 헌신하다
- task 혹사하다, 과업
- shoplifting 가게물건 훔치기
- alert 경고하다
- tend to 경향이 있다
- mentor 조언하다, 교사
- traction 견인
- ineffective 무능한, 효과가 없는
- sideline 출장 못하게 하다
- incompetent 무능한
- slipped 하락하다/ 미끄러지다
- value 중요성
- proverb 속담

  - And there are lessons to be learned from some of the countries that are **outperformin**g us right now.
    * 'outperform'은 'out'과 'perform'의 합성어로 '~를 능가하다'는 의미다. 이와 비슷한 구조의 단어는 '**outnumber**: ~보다 수적을 우세하다, **outmatch**: ~보다 한 수 위다, **outstanding**: 뛰어난, 두드러진'이 있다.

  - We tend to think we **should have taught** them better.
    * 'should have taught(p.p)'는 가정법적 용법(가정법 과거완료)으로

과거의 하지 못한 행위에 대한 후회를 나타낸다.
'**would have pp**: 주어에 의지가 있는 문장, **might have pp**: 추측, **could have pp**: 가능성'이다.

번역 미국과 일본의 교육 비교

마지막 뉴습니다. 오바마 대통령은 미국교육을 증진시키겠다고 다짐해왔습니다. 현재 우리를 능가하는 교육체제를 가진 일부 국가로부터 배울 교훈들이 있습니다.
일본의 경우 최고의 선생님을 모집하는데 초점을 맞추고 있습니다.
모집 후 이들이 얻어 온 존경과 경의를 가지고 대우합니다.
도쿄에서 셀리아 해튼기자가 전하는 '읽기, 쓰기 그리고 개혁' 시리즈입니다.

일본아이들이 아침 등교 후 처음 하는 일은 선생님께 인사하는 것입니다.
별 것 아닐지 몰라도 이 행동이 많은 것을 내포합니다.
이곳에서 존경은 노래제목이 아니라 일본 교육 시스템의 근간입니다.
일본교육은 수 십 년간 세계랭킹에서 높은 순위를 차지해 왔습니다.
선진국들 중에서 교육부문에 가장 적은 지출을 하고 있는 부분은 즉, 국내총생산(GDP)의 3.3%만을 차지하고 있는데 바로 학교교육에 관한 것이며 5%를 차지하는 미국과 비교됩니다.

그럼 어떻게 이렇게 적은 돈으로 큰 효과를 볼 수 있는 것일까요?
바로 최고의 선생님에게 투자하기 때문입니다.
"선생님들은 상당한 존경을 받습니다. 교직에 자신의 삶을 헌신할 것으로 예상됩니다."

교육시스템 전체가 선생님의 발전을 강조하는 쪽으로 맞춰집니다.
일본교육자들은 60세 정년퇴임하며 급여는 62,000달러 이상이며 미국이 53,000달러인 것과 비교됩니다.

하지만 그에 대한 대가로 선생님들은 아이들을 모범시민으로 만들어야 합니다.
예를 들어, 만약 한 학생이 가게물건을 훔치다 잡히면 보통 부모보다 그 학생의 선생님이 먼저 경고를 받습니다.
"학생들이 학교 밖에서 나쁜 짓을 하면, '우리들은 학생들을 더 잘 가르쳤어야 했다'라며 생각하는 경향이 있습니다."
교실 안에서 아이들은 책임감을 배웁니다.
학교 출입구에서 슬리퍼로 바꿔 신으며 스스로 학교를 청소합니다.
아이들은 순서를 정해 학급 친구들과 선생님에게 식사를 나눠줍니다.
그리고 모든 이들이 배식을 받기 전까진 아무도 밥을 먹지 않습니다.

선생님들은 또한 기간을 정해 서로 노트를 비교해 왔습니다.
이들의 책상은 심지어 한 공간에 모두 모여 있습니다.
"저는 60%정도는 학생들과 시간을 보내며 40%는 동료 교사들과 시간을 보냅니다."
정기적으로 수업을 녹화하여 고참 교사들이 신참 교사들에게 조언을 하는 것이 허용됩니다.
이것이 미국에서 관심을 끌고 있는 하나의 기법입니다.
그리고 일본에서 무능한 교사들은 해고되거나 수업을 못하게 하는 것이 아니라 폭넓은 재교육을 시킨다고 일본 교조 위원장이 설명합니다.
"무능한 교사를 이 시스템에 통과시키는 것은 불가능합니다."
이 모든 것에도 불구하고 중요한 국제올림피아드 성적이 모두 하락하고 있습니다.
일본은 2000년도에 국제수학올림피아드에서 1위를 차지했지만 2006년에는

6위로 떨어졌습니다. 하지만 25위인 미국보다는 훨씬 높습니다.
일본에서 바뀌고 있지 않는 것은 교육에 중요성을 둔다는 것입니다.
한 일본의 속담이 이것을 가장 잘 요약해줍니다.
"천 일간 공부하는 것보다 최고의 선생님과의 하루가 더 낫다."
도쿄에서 CBS 뉴스 셀리아 해튼기자였습니다.

Dictation

- And finally tonight, president Obama _____ _____ _____ _____ _____ _____ _____.
- And there are lessons _____ _____ _____ _____ _____ _____ _____ _____ _____ _____ _____ _____ _____ _____.
- Like Japan where _____ _____ _____ _____ _____ _____ _____,
  then treat them _____ _____ _____ _____ _____ _____ _____.
- Celia H atton _____ _____ _____ _____ _____: Reading, Writing and Reform.
- First thing in the morning, _____ _____ _____ _____ _____ _____.
- _____ _____ _____ _____ _____ _____ _____ _____.
- Here, respect _____ _____ _____ _____ _____ . _____ _____ _____ ,

Japan's school system _____ _____ _____ _____ ____ international rankings while spending the lowest amount ____ _____ _____ ____ _____, 3.3 % of Japan's gross domestic product or GDP goes _____ ____ _____ _____ _____ in the US.

- _____ _____ _____ _____ _____ _____ _____ _____ _____?

- _____ _____ _____ _____ _____.

- “ Teachers are given a good deal of respect. _____ _____ _____ _____ _____ _____.

- The whole system ____ _____ ____ ____ _____ _____ _____ ___ _____.”

- _____ _____ _____ _____ _____ _____ _____ with a salary of more than _____ _____ _____ _____ _____ _____ _____.

- But in return, teachers _____ _____ _____ _____ _____ _____ _____ _____.

- If a student _____ _____ _____, for example, the child's teacher ____ _____ _____ _____ ____ _____.

- “If our students do something wrong outside the school, _____ _____ _____ _____ _____ _____ _____ _____ _____ _____.”

- Inside the classroom, _____ _____ _____, _____ _____ _____ ____ _____ _____ _____ and cleaning the building themselves.

- Children ____ ____ ____ ____ ____ ____ ____ ____ and their teacher and no one takes a bite ____ ____ ____ ____.

- Teachers also ____ ____ ____ ____ ____ .

- ____ ____ ____ ____ ____ ____ ____ ____ ____ .

- "I spend 60 % of my time ____ ____ ____ ____ ____ ____ ____."

- Classes are regularly videotaped, ____ ____ ____ ____ ____ ____, a technique that's ____ ____ ____ ____ ____.

- ____ ____ ____ ____ ____ ____ ____ ____,

- They're given extensive retraining, ____ ____ ____ ____ ____ ____ ____ .

- " It's impossible for someone ____ ____ ____ ____ ____ ____ ____ ____."

- Despite all this, ____ ____ ____ ____ ____ ____ ____ ____ .

- Japan topped international math rankings in 2000, ____ ____ ____ ____ ____ ____, ____ ____ ____ ____ ____ ____ ____ ____ .

- What hasn't changed in Japan ____ ____ ______ ____ ____ _____,

  best summed up ___ ____ ____ ______ ,

  " better than a thousand days ___ ____ ___   _____ ____ _____

  ____ ______ _______ ."

  Celia Hatton, CBS News, Tokyo.

21

Restoring sight to the blind

And new hope for restoring sight to the blind.

From ABC News headquarters, this is ABC World News with Diane Sawyer.

And finally tonight, what could be a major development for damaged eyes.

Can they be coaxed into repairing themselves?

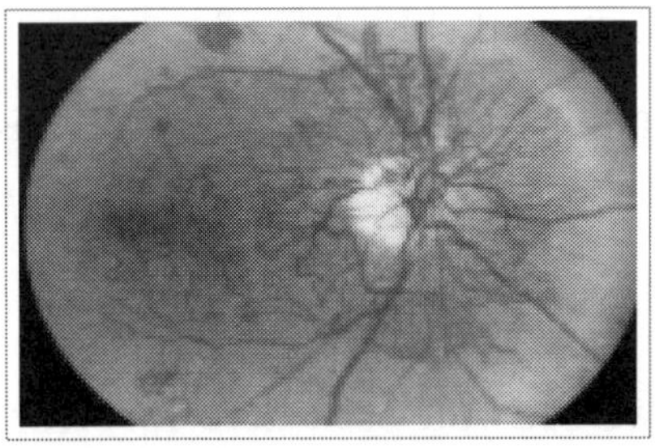

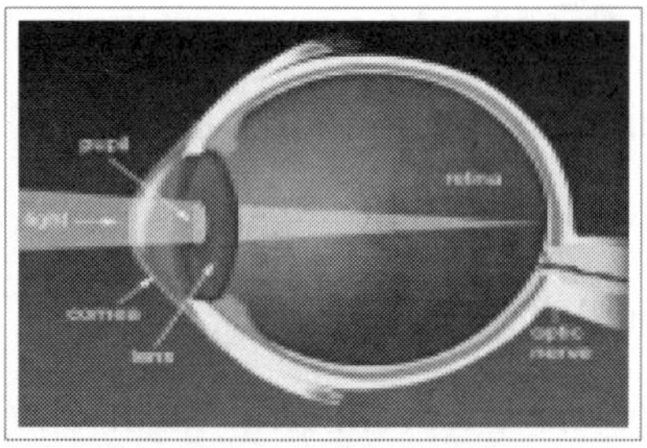

The news from Andrea Canning.

For people who see the world like this every day, a breakthrough.

Until now, there was little hope for the 10 million people who suffer from corneal blindness caused by infection, injury, and genetics.

The best option, a corneal transplant, but hard to get with a shortage of donors and requiring a lifetime of drugs to fend off rejection.

Now doctors have opened a whole new door.
An artificial cornea made of human collagen.
Almost like a contact lens sewn into your eye.
It actually coaxes the cornea to re-grow natural cells and nerves restoring sight.
“It does not appear that there are downsides because none of our patients showed any signs of rejection.”
It's just one of many recent breakthroughs.
This year, doctors were able to grow corneas by using patients' own stem cells.
This Cincinnati boy born without irises could only see in black and white until doctors implanted a silicone iris implant that allowed him to see vivid colors.

A tiny telescope implant allowed this man suffering from macular degeneration to see for the first time in years.
“I think this should give great hope to people with blindness.”
Potentially making this the decade when millions will finally see like this.
Andrea canning, ABC News, New York.
And wouldn't that be great?
Hope you have a wonderful night and that we see you back here for World News again tomorrow night.

Words and Idioms

- coaxed 구슬려 시키다
  - She **coaxed** the horse into coming a little closer.
    그녀는 말을 구슬려 좀 더 가까이 오게 했다.
- corneal 각막
  - Long-term use of contact lenses could cause **corneal** damage.
    콘택트렌즈를 장기간 사용하면 각막에 손상을 일으킬 수 있다.
- genetics 유전
- fend off 막아내다
  - She managed to **fend off** questions about new tax increases.
    그녀는 새로운 세금 인상에 관한 질문들을 간신히 피했다.
- rejection 거부반응
- sewn sew의 과거 과거분사
  - These shirts are ripped. I'd like to have them **sewn** up.
    이 셔츠가 찢어졌는데, 꿰매 주세요.
- coaxes 구슬리다
  - The director **coaxed** a brilliant performance out of the cast.
    감독은 배우들을 잘 다뤄 놀라운 연기를 뽑아냈다.
- downside 불리한 면
  - That's the **downside** of the rush to put every kid online.
    그것은 모든 아이들을 온라인상으로 몰아가는 것의 부정적인 단면이다.
- stem cells 줄기세포

- iris 홍채

- macular degeneration 시력감퇴

  - And new hope for **restoring sight** to the blind

    * "restore sight"는 '시력을 회복하다'로 동의어로는 'regain[recover] one's sight'가 있으며 반의어로는 'lose one's sight'가 있다.

  - A tiny telescope implant allowed this man suffering from **macular degeneration.**

    * "macular degeneration"은 '시력감퇴'이며 망막의 중심부인 황반부에 이상이 발생하여 글 읽기나 근거리 작업이 어려워진다. 주로 노인들에게 많이 발생하지만 외상, 염증 등에 의해서도 발생할 수 있다.

번역 시력장애 치료

시력장애를 치료해줄 새로운 희망적인 방법이 나왔습니다.
ABC 월드뉴스의 다이나 소어입니다.
오늘 마지막 뉴스는 손상된 눈을 위한 큰 발전일 수도 있는 것에 대한 것인데요.
손상된 눈이 스스로 치료되는 것이 가능할까요?
앤드리아 캐닝기자가 소식을 전합니다.

매일 이렇게 세상을 보는 사람들에게 있어서 돌파구적인 소식이 있습니다.
지금까지 천만 명의 각막 시력장애를 겪은 사람들에게는 거의 희망이 없었습니다.
이 시력장애는 감염, 상해, 유전적 요인에 의해 발생합니다.

각막 이식이 최고의 치료방법이었습니다.
하지만 각막 기증자는 부족하고 이식된다고 해도 거부반응을 막기 위해 평생 약을 복용해야 합니다.

지금 의사들은 완전히 새로운 세계로의 문을 열고 있습니다.
인간 콜라겐으로 만든 인공 각막이 그것입니다.
콘택츠렌즈와 거의 비슷하며 눈에 이식됩니다.
실제로 인공 각막이 자연적으로 세포와 신경을 재생산시켜 시력을 회복시킵니다.
"부작용은 없는 것으로 보입니다.
거부반응을 보이는 환자가 전혀 없기 때문입니다."

이것은 단지 많은 획기적인 사건들 중 하나일 뿐입니다.
올해 의사들은 환자의 줄기세포를 이용해 각막을 만들어낼 수 있었습니다.
신시니티에 사는 이 소년은 태어날 때부터 홍채가 없어서 흑백만 볼 수 있었습니다.
하지만 의사들이 실리콘 홍채 이식을 해서 이 소년은 생생한 색상을 보게 되었습니다.

작은 망원경을 눈에 이식시켜 황반변성을 겪고 있던 이 남자는 수년 만에 처음으로 볼 수 있게 되었습니다.
"저는 이것이 시력장애를 겪는 사람들에게 큰 희망을 줄 거라 생각됩니다."
아마도 이것은 수백만 명이 마침내 이렇게 볼 수 있는 10년을 만들어 줄 것입니다.
뉴욕에서 ABC 뉴스 앤드리아 캐닝이었습니다.
대단하지 않습니까?
좋은 밤 보내시고 내일 밤 월드 뉴스에서 다시 뵙겠습니다.

Dictation

- ______ ______ ______ ______ ______ ______ ______ ______ ______.
- From ABC News headquarters, this is ABC World News with Diane Sawyer.
- ______ ______ ______, what could be a major development ______ ______ ______.
- Can they ______ ______ ______ ______ ______?
- ______ ______ ______ ______ ______.
- For people ______ ______ ______ ______ ______ ______ ______ ______, a breakthrough.
- Until now, there was little hope ______ ______ ______ ______ ______ who suffer ______ ______ ______ caused by infection, ______, ______ ______ .
- The best option, a corneal transplant, ______ ______ ______ ______ ______ ______ ______ ______ ______
  and requiring a lifetime of drugs ______ ______ ______ ______ .
- ______ ______ ______ ______ ______ ______ ______ ______.
- An artificial cornea ______ ______ ______ ______ .
- Almost like ______ ______ ______ ______ ______ ______ ______.
- ______ ______ ______ ______ ______ ______ re-grow natural cells ______ ______ ______ ______.

- "It does not appear _____ _______ ______ ______ because none of our patients ______ ______ ____ _____ ________."
- It's just _____ _____ ______ ______ _________.
- This year, doctors ______ _____ _____ _____ ______ _____ _____ ______ _____ ______ _______ .
- This Cincinnati boy born _____ ______ ______ ______ _____ ______ _____ ____ _____ ______ ______ implanted a silicone iris implant ____ ______ _____ ____ _______ _____ _______.
- A tiny telescope _____ ____ ______ _____ ______ _____ ______ ________ to see for the first time in years.
- "I think this should give great hope ____ _____ _______ _______."
- Potentially making ______ _____ _______ _______ _____ ______ _______ _____ _______ _______.
- _____ _______ _____, ABC News, New York.
- _____ _______ _____ ______ _______?
_____ ______ ______ _____ ______ _______ and that we see you back here for World News again tomorrow night.

22

Finland, the best education system in the world

And education nation. A place where teachers and students have stunning success. So what's their secret?

For days, we've been hearing about the ideal education system in the world.

Finland, educators talk about Finland all the time.

So much so in fact, we decided to go there and see what makes their system so good.

Here tonight, our education correspondent Rehema Ellis.

Finland, population five million, about the size of the Atlanta metro area.

But don't let size fool you. Finland is a global success.

Home to cell phone giant Nokia, Finns are known for their love of coffee, state-supported health care and the best education system in the world.
15-year-old Onie Olsen is a typical Finnish student.
He balances school work with play.

But school time is very focused and it shows.
Internationally, Finnish students rank No.1 overall in science and math.
US kids rank 17th in science and 24th in math.
“Can you say what percentage of your students drop out from school?” “In our school, nobody.”
Nationwide, the high school dropout rate is 2% versus 25% in the US.
But it wasn't always this way.
40 years ago, Finland was a poor nation depending on agriculture.
Its leaders envisioned a brighter future in technology.
The nation decided the way to get there was with a better educated workforce.
It took a generation to do it.

Finland's blueprint included a tough national curriculum.
Masters degrees for all teachers with up to three teachers per class.
Two, focus on instruction. The third, works with students who are struggling.
The result? There's no such thing as a failing school in Finland.
Officials say Finland has a collective national will to educate all students.
“Have you got a cat?” There's a relax atmosphere in the classroom and continuity.
“I can be a better teacher when I teach them longer, for a longer period.”
Many students stay with the same teacher for several years.

"Use English as much as possible."

The average student speaks four languages including English.
And Finland spends about $3,000 less per people than American schools do.
So how do they achieve more?
Education experts credit involved parents.
"Do you push your son?" "Perhaps, sometimes. Yeah, to be honest, yes."
Equally important, they say, is the Finnish culture that values education.
A report out this month says 47% of America's teachers come from the bottom third of college graduates.
Finnish teachers come from the top 10% just like doctors and lawyers.
Finland's best and brightest are chosen to teach.
Rehema Ellis, NBC News, Hill sinking, Finland.

Words and Idioms

- envision 마음속에 그리다
  - They **envision** an equal society, free of poverty and disease.
    그들은 가난과 질병이 없는 평등한 사회를 마음속에 그리고 있다.
- collective 공통의
  - The union secured its demands through **collective** bargaining.
    노동조합은 단체교섭을 통해 그들의 요구사항을 관철했다.

• continuity 연속성

- The novel fails to achieve narrative **continuity.**
  그 소설은 이야기의 연속성 구현에 실패하고 있다.

- Home to cell phone giant Nokia, Finns **are known for** their love of coffee, state-supported health care and the best education system in the world.
  * be known 은 뒤에 오는 전치사에 따라 의미가 달라진다. be known for 는 '~로 알려지다(이유), be known as는 '~로 알려져 있다(자격)', be known to(행위 대상)는 '~에게 알려져 있다'이며, be known by는 '~로 알 수 있다'이다.

- Education experts **credit** involved parents.
  * credit은 '~ 에게(공로, 명예)돌리다'는 의미이다.

번역 세계 최고의 핀란드 교육시스템

교육 국가입니다. 교사와 학생들이 놀라운 성과를 거두는 곳입니다. 비결이 무엇일까요?
수 일간 전 세계의 이상적인 교육 시스템에 관한 소식을 들었습니다.
핀란드의 교사들은 언제나 핀란드에 대해 이야기 합니다.
이에 따라 사실 그곳에 가서 무엇 때문에 교육 시스템이 그렇게 좋은지 확인하기로 결심했습니다.
오늘 저녁, 본사의 교육 전문기자 레헤마 엘리스가 보도합니다.

핀란드 인구는 5백만 명으로 미국의 애틀란타 수도권 정도의 크기입니다.
규모를 보고 핀란드를 우습게보지 마시기 바랍니다. 핀란드는 세계적인 성공을 이뤘습니다.
휴대폰의 거대기업인 노키아의 본고장이고, 핀란드인들은 커피 애호가이며 국가지원의 보건의료 및 세계 최고 수준의 교육시스템을 누리는 것으로 잘 알려져 있습니다.
15세인 오니 올슨은 전형적인 핀란드 학생입니다.
그는 학교 공부와 놀이에 균형을 맞춥니다.

한편 수업 시간에는 매우 집중력을 발휘하는 모습을 보여줍니다.
국제적으로 핀란드 학생들은 전반적으로 과학과 수학에서 1위를 차지합니다.
미국 학생들은 과학에서는 17위, 수학에서는 24위를 차지했습니다.
"학교에서 퇴학하는 학생들은 몇 퍼센트인가요?", "저희 학교에는 한 명도 없습니다."
전국적으로 고등학교 중퇴율은 2%이며 미국의 25%와 비교됩니다.
그러나 늘 이렇지는 않았습니다.
약 40년 전 핀란드는 농업에 의존하는 가난한 국가였습니다.
국가 지도자들이 기술 부문에 밝은 미래를 계획했습니다.
국가는 그 계획을 이룰 방법으로 제대로 교육 받은 인력이 뒷받침 돼야 한다고 생각했습니다.
이를 위해 한 세대의 시간이 걸렸습니다.

핀란드의 청사진에는 견실한 국가적 커리큘럼이 포함되어 있었습니다.
모든 교사들은 석사학위를 소지해야 하고 교실마다 교사가 최대 3명이 있어야 했습니다.
두 번째는 교육에 집중하는 것이고, 세 번째는 애쓰고 있는 학생들과 함께 공부하는 것입니다.
그 결과는? 핀란드에는 부실한 학교가 없어졌습니다.
관계자들에 따르면 핀란드는 모든 학생을 교육시키려는 국가적 차원의 공동의지가 있다고 합니다.

"고양이 한 마리가 있나요 ?" 교실에는 편안한 분위기가 돌며 지속성을 지닙니다.
"학생들을 오랫동안 더 오랜 기간 가르칠 때 더 좋은 교사가 될 수 있습니다."
학생들 다수가 수년 간 같은 선생님과 함께 합니다.
"가능한 많이 영어를 사용하세요."

보통의 학생은 영어를 포함해서 4개 국어를 구사합니다.
또한, 핀란드는 미국 학교보다 한 사람당 약 $3,000적게 사용합니다.
그렇다면 그들은 어떻게 더 많은 것을 성취하는 걸까요?
교육 전문가들은 학부모들의 참여 덕분이라고 합니다.
"아들에게 강요하시나요?", "아마도 가끔이요. 솔직히 그렇습니다."
이와 동등하게 핀란드 문화에서는 교육에 가치를 둔다는 사실도 중요합니다.
이번 달에 나온 한 보고서에 따르면 미국 교사들의 47%가 대학 졸업생들 중 하위 1/3에 해당합니다.
반면 핀란드 교사들은 의사 및 변호사처럼 상위 10% 출신입니다.
핀란드에서 가장 탁월하고 똑똑한 학생들이 교직을 선택합니다.
핀란드 헬싱키에서 NBC 뉴스, 레헤마 엘리스 기자였습니다.

Dictation

- ______ ______ ______. A place where teachers and students ______ ______ ______. ______ ______ ______ ______?
- For days, we've been hearing ______ ______ ______ ______ ______ ______ ______ ______.

- ______, ______ ______ ______ ______ ______ ______ ______.
- ____ _____ ____ _____ _____, we decided to go there and see ____ ____ _____ _____ _____ ______.
- _____ _____ , _____ ______ ______ Rehema Ellis .
- Finland, ______ _____ _____ , _____ _____ ______ ______ ______ ______ ______ ______ .
- But don't let size fool you . _____ ____ _____ _____ ______ .
- Home to cell phone giant Nokia, Finns are known _____ _____ _____ ____ ______ ,
  _______ ______ _____ _____ _____ _____ ______ ______ in the world.
- ______ ______ ______ _____ _____ _______ _____ ________.
- ______ ______ _______ ______ ______ ______.
- ______ _____ _____ _____ ______ ______ ______ ______ ______.
- Internationally, Finnish students rank No.1 _____ _____ ______ _____ ______.
- ______ ______ _____ ______ ______ _______ ______ _____ ____ _____.
- "Can you say _____ _______ _____ ______ _____ _____ _____ ______ ______?" "In our school, nobody."
- ______, ______ _____ ______ ______ ______ ____ _____ ______

_____ _____ _____ _____.

- _____ _____ _____ _____ _____ _____.
- 40 years ago, Finland _____ _____ _____ _____ _____ _____ _____.
- _____ _____ _____ _____ _____ _____ in technology.
- The nation decided the way to get there _____ _____ _____ _____ _____ _____.
- _____ _____ _____ _____ _____ _____ _____.
- _____ _____ _____ _____ _____ _____ _____.
- Masters degrees for all teachers _____ _____ _____ _____ _____ _____ _____.
- Two, focus on instruction. The third, _____ _____ _____ _____ _____ _____.
- The result? There's no such thing _____ _____ _____ _____ _____ _____.

  Officials say Finland has _____ _____ _____ _____ _____ _____ _____ _____.
- "Have you got a cat?" There's _____ _____ _____ _____ _____ _____ _____ _____ .
- "I can be a better teacher _____ _____ _____ _____ _____, _____ _____ _____ _____."

- Many students stay ______ ______ ______ ______ ______ ______ ______.
- "______ ______ ______ ______ ______ ______."
- The average student ______ ______ ______ ______ ______.
- And Finland spends ______ ______ ______ ______ ______ ______ ______ ______ ______.
- ______ ______ ______ ______ ______ ______?
- ______ ______ ______ ______ ______.
- "______ ______ ______ ______ ______?" "Perhaps, sometimes. ______, ______ ______ ______, ______."
- Equally important, they say, ______ ______ ______ ______ ______ ______ ______.
- A report out ______ ______ ______ ______ ______ ______ ______ come from the bottom third of college graduates.
- ______ ______ ______ ______ ______ ______ ______ just like doctors and lawyers.
- ______ ______ ______ ______ ______ ______ ______ ______.

  Rehema Ellis, NBC News, Hill sinking, Finland.

저자약력

박노철 · 세종대학교 영어영문학과 번역학전공(박사)
· 몬터레이 통번역대학원 수료
· 현) 경인여자대학 관광영어과 겸임교수

■ 주요 저서
· 비유언어 번역방법

뉴 통번역연습

2011년 2월 25일 초판1쇄 인쇄
2011년 2월 28일 초판1쇄 발행

저자와의
협의하에
인지생략

저 자 박 노 철
펴낸이 임 순 재
펴낸곳 한올출판사
등록 제11-403호
121 - 849
주 소 서울시 마포구 성산동 133-3 한올빌딩 3층
전 화 (02)376-4298(대표)
팩 스 (02)302-8073
홈페이지 www.hanol.co.kr
e-메 일 hanol@hanol.co.kr
정 가 16,000원(CD 포함)

■ ISBN 978-89-94948-00-3